LOWELL HARDIN

LOWELL HARDIN: MENTOR EXTRAOR-DINAIRE

EDITED BY
LARRY L. MURDOCK
THOMAS W. HERTEL
AND GEBISA EJETA

PURDUE UNIVERSITY PRESS · WEST LAFAYETTE, INDIANA

978-1-62671-172-3 (paperback)
978-1-61249-914-7 (epub)
978-1-61249-915-4 (epdf)

Cover: Lowell Hardin, 87, ready for takeoff in Larry and Susie Murdock's 1928 Travel Air 4000 open cockpit biplane. During the 30-minute hop up to Lake Freeman and back, the smile never left his face. He kept this photo on his desk ever after.

Contents

Foreword

Tom Hertel and Larry Murdock

Lowell Hardin's gift was to inspire others, to encourage and motivate them, and to open doors. He helped people quietly, in the background, and never called attention to what he did. Those of us who knew Lowell and were mentored by him owe him an unpayable debt. Larry Murdock, Tom Hertel and Gebisa Ejeta, continually reminded of the benefits and helping hand Lowell gave them, wish to pass his gifts on to those less lucky than ourselves—those who didn't know him.

For those who had the good fortune of knowing him, it will be heartwarming to read the memories of others. In this modest volume, we have gathered stories and anecdotes about Lowell from individuals whose lives were touched by him. Those accounts of what Lowell did for and with them will add to the gifts this remarkable man gave to the world, and maybe, in a small way, will influence another generation.

This would please Lowell, we think, and it will also be a way of our saying thanks. That's where the authors of these pieces come in. Lowell was a significant influence in their lives or careers. The portraits or sketches they took the time to write help us recognize and honor him. We hope this little book highlights and preserves the legacy of this rare and remarkable man, and keeps his memory from being lost to the teeth of time.

Preface

Gebisa Ejeta

*Introductory remarks for the symposium on "Green Revolutions"
held at Purdue University on the occasion of Lowell Hardin's
90th birthday, 2007.*

O n this cold and crisp December morning, we have come from far
and near to honor a special person, to hold up with pride and grati-
tude a respected colleague, a loyal ambassador of goodwill for Purdue University and the State of Indiana, and a stalwart of the international
agricultural research and development community. Yes, we are here to pay
tribute to the life and work of Lowell Stewart Hardin, Professor Emeritus of
Agricultural Economics at Purdue University.

We will be honoring this very unassuming and humble man who many in
this room feel honored to have known, a man who many here and perhaps
hundreds of others elsewhere will point to as a great mentor, a trusted confi-
dant, a wise counselor, and a visionary leader. This is a man with a very common beginning and upbringing who used his God-given talents and the opportunities afforded him along the way to a very uncommon end. Lowell
Hardin was born on November 16, 1917, to a family of faith in Henry County,
Indiana. He was reared on a general livestock farm in a lifestyle perhaps typical of such a family at the time. As to the college he attended, Lowell makes a
rather matter-of-fact statement in his memoir: "Though some of our church
friends went to Earlham College, we were farm kids. Farm kids studied agriculture. Purdue was the agriculture college, so all three Hardin kids, Lowell,
Russell, and Helen, went to Purdue."

Lowell graduated from Purdue University with a degree in Animal Science,
a few courses in Agronomy and some extracurricular experiences, such as

managing editor of the *Purdue Exponent* and serving as a field inspector for Indiana Crop Improvement Association. He attended graduate school at Cornell University. Upon completing his graduate program in 1943, he returned to Purdue as a faculty member in the Department of Agricultural Economics, moving through the ranks initially as Instructor and then as Assistant, Associate and Full Professor, and eventually serving as Head of Department.

After 22 years on the faculty, this local boy from Indiana began his uncommon journey in 1965 by accepting a new assignment as Senior Agricultural Officer, at the Office of Vice President, in the International Division of the Ford Foundation. This unusual and bold move from West Lafayette, Indiana, to Manhattan, New York, was emboldened by heavy nudging from none other than his own partner, Mary, the mother of his three young children, whom he describes as "a professor's daughter who was more enlightened, more worldly, and unafraid to discover the greater world around her than he, the Hoosier farm boy, was at the time." This single, one-time decision was transformational for the Hardins, their young children, and, as it turned out, for the rest of the world as well.

Lowell had a great career as a Purdue professor, where he excelled in the more conventional functions of a faculty member in his department, serving as a teacher, researcher, administrator, and in disseminating knowledge of Farm Management to the farmers of Indiana. But he received global recognition of great distinction after leaving his faculty position at Purdue to work for the Ford Foundation. It was after joining Ford and through programs and partnerships that he created there that his sharp mind, great wisdom, enviable organizational and leadership skills, great work ethic, and almost saintly interpersonal relations earned him a truly iconic status and respect for what ended up to be a lifelong service and dedication to humanity in the field of international agricultural research and development.

Reputations earned at Ford and *ex-officio* capacities as a representative of one of the two major foundations that supported international research and development in those days, Lowell served as a member and Chair of Trustees of numerous organizations, including the Agricultural Development Council, ADC, New York (1962–1966); the International Center for the Improvement of Wheat and Maize in Mexico, CIMMYT (1966–1972); the International Agricultural Development Service, ADS, New York (1968–1972); the

International Center for Tropical Agriculture, CIAT, Colombia (1967–1972); the International Center for Agricultural Research in the Dry Areas, ICARDA, Syria (1979–1985); the International Service for National Agricultural Research, ISNAR, The Hague (1979–1984); the International Food Policy Research Institute, IFPRI, Washington D.C. (1980–1987); and Winrock International of Morrilton, Arkansas (1985–1993).

In addition, he served as member or chair of External Management Reviews of many of the same Centers at different times. Lowell also served as member of the Agricultural Board of the National Academy of Sciences (1966–1972) as well as member of the National Research Council Panel on Agricultural Sustainability and the Environment (1990–1993) and Chair of the National Research Council Panel for Collaborative Research Support of USAID's Sustainable Agriculture and Natural Resource Management Program (1990–1991). Furthermore, Lowell joined or led numerous delegations to a number of countries in Asia, Latin America, and Africa, including Brazil, Mexico, Colombia, Peru, Ethiopia, Kenya, South Africa, India, Pakistan, Bangladesh, Philippines, Japan, and many others.

Many of the organizations listed above were either coming on to the scene or were in their formative years at the time. So Lowell was one of the architects who created and nurtured many of these centers. He was one of the early visionaries who promoted the cause of organized agricultural sciences to address the concerns of hunger and poverty. He was a member of the "greatest generation of science" folks who created the concept of International Agricultural Research and Development and put in place machinery such as the Consultative Group on International Agricultural Research (CGIAR) for their governance and sustenance. As a member of several boards of trustees, he was one of the leaders who encouraged good governance and provided guidance to help minimize risks. As external advisor, he crafted ways for enhancing management efficiency, gaining financial discipline, and increasing programmatic effectiveness. Many who served with him acknowledge his attention to detail, his deep understanding of the issues, his emphases on governance, need for financial discipline, partnerships, science quality, and push for deliverables. These are themes that he continues to champion to this day.

While at the Ford Foundation, Lowell funded programs in many of these centers as well as in more bilateral programs of many other countries. He offered scholarships that educated so many young professionals in many developing countries. He mentored many of these professionals on their return to their countries, whether they held academic or policy slots in their governments. In sum, the institutions that benefited from Lowell's contributions are many. The contributions are varied. The impact has been huge. Yet, Lowell never enumerates those contributions; he doesn't even claim any. He is quick to credit those achievements to others.

Through the years, Lowell also remained an active participant of his scientific organizations, serving successively as Secretary-Treasurer, Vice President, and President of the American Agricultural Economics Association over a period of 10 years. For his many services and scholastic contributions, Lowell received several recognitions, including Fellow of the American Agricultural Economic Association and Fellow of the American Association for the Advancement of Sciences, and several citations and awards. Lowell returned to Purdue University in 1982, after his retirement from the Ford Foundation, and gave us 25 more years of incredible service of teaching, advising, and mentoring.

So, as a small committee of friends gathered to plan a celebration for his 90th birthday, and to thank him for almost 70 years of professional service, we wanted to put together a program that would both honor Lowell's contributions and draw attention to issues important to him. We also wanted to do something that would please Lowell and Mary.

However, we reasoned that pleasing the Hardins meant that the planned festivity and program should be modest and not excessive; substantive and not petty; it should be more intellectual and less emotive; it should be about less of the past and more of the now and tomorrow. Above all it can't all be about aggrandizing Lowell, as this Lifelong Professor will want it to be less about him and more about an educational opportunity for all. This man of unusual humility and piety will want this to be an experience in retrospective reflection that may energize prospective visioning.

So we selected a topic in an area of international development that we considered timely. We also looked for the best authorities in the field among Lowell's mentees to speak on them. We selected the theme "Green Revolutions" for the following reasons: Through his long and productive career, both by design and by good fortune, Lowell has witnessed all of the significant agricultural

revolutions of the 20th century. He has been a leader and interested participant in each of them. Hybrid corn hit the market as Lowell was entering college. In my opinion this was the first "green revolution," though the term was
not created at the time. As a graduate student at Cornell and later as a faculty
member at Purdue, he witnessed the unfolding of a remarkable agricultural
revolution advanced in this country through the great agro-industry complex that this scientific discovery spurred. He was among the leaders who en-
abled the "Asian Green Revolution" to take place with lessons from the U.S.
corn revolution. He was an active participant when the ills of the "Asian Green
Revolution" were debated and when Gordon Conway and others proposed
terms and concepts such as "the Doubly Green Revolution" as to what the
next generation of agricultural revolution needed to be. Lowell was also an
enthusiastic participant in the dialogue about the potential of the "Biotechnology Revolution" that came about in the last two decades. As he is fond of
saying, he doesn't quite understand the science, but he can see the possibili-
ties. Finally, interest is perking up again when he hears of the initiative currently underway at the "Alliance for Green Revolution in Africa" under the
auspices of the Rockefeller Foundation and the Bill and Melinda Gates Foundation. In other words, Green Revolutions, as mechanisms for impacting lives
through the agricultural sciences, have been Lowell Hardin's vocation and av-
ocation for nearly 70 years.

As to our distinguished speakers, each is a self-acknowledged mentee of
Lowell Hardin. In each of these great people we would see the very attributes
that we liked and respected in Lowell. Each is very articulate, very thoughtful.
They are all visionaries, dreamers, and scholars, like Lowell. Above all, with
over 150 years of combined international development experience, they have
earned the reputation as great leaders in international agriculture with collective wisdom, à la Lowell Hardin. Like Lowell, they have been loyal servants,
generous with their time, and willing to share their wisdom and knowledge
for the cause of humanity. We thought if we asked, they would accept our invitation to come and be part of this function, and they all did. Each covered
their own expenses to get here to honor Lowell.

At the end of this morning, it is my wish that we will all have a "Lowell
Hardin moment." We will have looked back retrospectively to seek lessons
from the past, and gaze forward to see what it will mean for the future. I am

hopeful that for this day, we will have been recharged and energized, and will have been empowered and made hopeful.

Above all, I hope we will have felt good that we have taken a moment to say "Thank You!" to a loyal Boilermaker and a servant of global agriculture, designer of programs, architect of institutions, and builder of people, to a simple farm boy from Henry County, Indiana, who went on to develop uncommon insights to complex issues that affected lives in faraway places in a world that he never knew existed. God blessed Lowell with good health and with ageless intellect and wisdom for a good reason. Through him and his work, the world has been made a better place. And that is cause for celebration. Thank you.

People come to see you for various reasons. It may be for advice, or for information, encouragement, sympathy, or even just for moments of companionship. But when the purpose of the meeting has been achieved, it should be terminated, in a kind and friendly way for sure, but firmly. Doing so shows respect for your visitor, and for yourself.

PART 1

Ford Foundation and International Agricultural Research

Wally Falcon

Such was the span of Lowell's influence.

Walter Falcon is former deputy director of the Center on Food Security and the Environment, former director of the Freeman Spogli Institute for International Studies, and Farnsworth professor of International Agricultural Policy and Economics at Stanford University (Emeritus).

In 1972, Falcon moved from Harvard University to Stanford University's Food Research Institute, where he served as professor of economics and director until 1991. From 1991 to 1998, he directed the Freeman Spogli Institute for International Studies, and from 1998 to 2007 he co-directed the Center for Environmental Science and Policy. He has also served as senior associate dean for the social sciences, a member of the academic senate, and twice as a member of the University's Advisory Board.

Falcon has consulted with numerous international organizations, and has been a trustee of Winrock International and chairman of the board of the International Rice Research Institute (IRRI) and the International Center for Wheat and Maize Improvement (CIMMYT). Falcon became a Fellow of the American Association for the Advancement of Science in 1991. Falcon was cited as the outstanding 1958 graduate of Iowa State University in 1989 and in 1992 he was awarded the prestigious Bintang Jasa Utama medal of merit by the government of Indonesia for 25 years of assistance with that country's development effort. His recent co-authored papers have analyzed the effects of El Nino on Asian agriculture; Mexican agricultural policy; food price volatility; and biofuels.

Falcon received a B.S. in Agricultural Economics at Iowa State University in 1958, an M.A. in Economics at Harvard University in 1960, and a Ph.D. in Economics from Harvard University in 1962.

I, too, am one of Lowell's boys. He was my mentor and friend for more than 50 years. Ironically, however, he was not my major professor, I never took a class from him, I was never at Purdue, and I never worked for him! But such was the span of Lowell's influence, and I was a lucky beneficiary.

I first met Lowell in the mid-1960s. These were heady times for all of us. Lowell had joined David Bell (a former Harvard professor of mine who actually introduced Lowell to me) at the Ford Foundation. At that time, the Foundation was a major positive force within developing countries, and especially in bringing the Green Revolution seed and water technologies to South Asia. I was a young Harvard Assistant Professor at the time, on leave for a two-year stint as the agriculture and irrigation advisor with the Pakistan Planning Commission. These were wonderful years, and I remember well working with Lowell and Norman Borlaug on Pakistan's wheat program. Usually we were of one voice, but Norm was never a great lover of economists. When he argued that, despite the doubling of wheat yields, the wheat procurement price also needed to be doubled, we took exception. And this in turn caused Norm to proclaim: "You damned economists are always trying to kill my program!"

After returning to the faculty at Harvard, I remained in close touch with Lowell. Maybe he saw it as an opportunity to help an Iowa farm boy, or perhaps as an obligation—in any event, I was most grateful for his counsel. Although Harvard at that time was awash in development economists, I was the only one with agricultural credentials. John D. Black had retired, and J. Kenneth Galbraith—actually hired as Harvard's agricultural economist!—had long since moved on to other areas. In some fundamental sense, Lowell was my big brother during those years. He helped me figure out the do's and don'ts of academia, the ins and outs of getting research grants, and what research topics were important and not just interesting.

When I moved to Stanford in 1972 as Director of the (then) Food Research Institute, Lowell, at least in spirit, made the move with me. Academic departments don't just run themselves, and Lowell was again a wonderful source of informed, practical advice. During the 1980s, I also began to see Lowell in a quite different light. He was a dominant player in the formation and operation of the Consultative Group for International Agricultural Research (CGIAR), and he served on the Board of Trustees of many of the Centers within that group. In my first assignment ever as a Trustee, I was fortunate to join a board on which Lowell was also a member. He was a real pro, unequivocally the best board member with whom I have ever served, and a great teacher by example.

Lowell's style was to show up a couple of days prior to the meeting and simply walk around and talk with scientists and staff at all levels. In board meetings themselves, he was informed, low-key, courtly, and always full of positive suggestions. But he also had a steely toughness that Directors-General soon learned to respect. Because of his diligence, hard work, and style, I never saw him lose a board issue of significance. One of his greatest assets was in reminding everyone of what was a board decision, and which decisions resided with management.

As we grew older, and the 21st century arrived, our relationship evolved. He sought my advice, and I sought his. I would describe our interchanges as personal, professional, and inspirational. One of Lowell's core qualities was his interest in families. I can never remember a conversation with him in which either the first or second topic did not focus on my family. It was none of the "How's your family?" "Oh, they are fine" variety either. He wanted full chapter and verse on where everyone was and what they were doing. Our elder son was developmentally and physically disabled, and early on, my wife and I made the decision that he (Phillip) would live at home. Lowell was great with Phillip, and he had tons of helpful advice for us about traveling and living abroad with him.

On the professional front, Lowell continued to keep abreast of nearly everything related to international agriculture well into his 90s. I called him on dozens of occasions wanting to know this thing or that, and his replies never disappointed on what was happening, and more importantly, why. I always sent him my research papers—hoping he would like them, but knowing full well that if he didn't, he would tell me. And I always knew if there was a soft spot in my argument, Lowell would find it.

Finally, Lowell was—and still is—inspirational to me. When I turned 80, Lowell remarked something about life finally getting interesting. And I long to do in my 90s what Lowell did in his—give a rousing departmental seminar.

Be encouraging, but don't make promises. If you are able to intervene and help in some active way, do so quietly, sub rosa, but never talk about what you did.

Werner Kiene

You will always be one of Hardin's boys.

After undergraduate training in Austria at the University of Natural Resources and Life Sciences in Vienna, Werner Kiene obtained his M.Sc. and Ph.D. degrees in Agricultural Economics at Michigan State University. He joined the Ford Foundation Headquarters in New York as an Assistant Program Officer in 1972.

During his 10 years with the Foundation he also served as Program Advisor for Agriculture in the Foundation's Office for North Africa and subsequently for the West Africa Office. After a year at the International Institute for Applied Systems Analysis (IIASA) he spent 10 years on various assignments with the German Development Assistance Organization GTZ (now GIZ). In 1994, he joined the UN-World Food Programme (WFP) in Rome as the Founding Director of its Office of Evaluation. From 1997 on he was WFP's Country Director in Bangladesh. During this time, he served also as UN-Resident Coordinator. In the fall of 2000, he moved to Washington, D.C., as WFP Representative to the Bretton Woods Institutions in efforts to better align food aid with broader development and emergency programs.

From 2004 on, Dr. Kiene served first as Member and then as Chairman of the World Bank's Inspection Panel that ensures compliance with the Bank's policies and procedures for social and environmental standards. After five years with the Panel, he took up assignments with similar objectives at the Inter-American Development Bank and at UNDP. During recent years, he has devoted some of his energies to governance of the international fair trade movement. His continued commitment to food and environmental concerns is manifested by his current position as Chairman of the Board of the London-based Marine Stewardship Council (MSC), a global organization devoted to ensuring sustainable fishery practices in the world's oceans. He has held this office since 2013.

F irst a great smile. Then, "Please sit down and tell me about yourself." This was how my first encounter with Lowell Hardin started in the summer of 1972 at his office on the sixth floor of the Ford Foundation building in New York. I had come to this interview with the usual trepidations of a young academic encountering a star of his profession, yet Lowell knew how to quickly break the ice. We had an interesting conversation that was the first in more than four decades of learning from him.

A couple of months later, I started my assignment with him as an Assistant Program Officer in the Foundation's International Division. Lowell involved me in all aspects of his exciting work: There were many activities related to operationalizing the grand ideas of the Consultative Group for International Agricultural Research (CGIAR), with stimulating meetings with colleagues from the Rockefeller Foundation and other partners committed to this venture; preparing crucial inputs into organizing the initial CGIAR meetings at the World Bank in Washington, and preparing funding strategies. Another important program component that Lowell drew me into was the support to the "Rural Social Sciences in the Third World," a path-breaking initiative complementing the bio-technical focus of the early CGIAR programs. Lowell's enthusiasm for all the aspects of his work was infectious and has continued to inspire me throughout my own career.

The various facets of Lowell's mentoring

Lowell was a fantastic mentor, not only for developing strategies that are consistent with one's values, but also for growing professionally. Although my mandate was to assist him in all his activities, he insisted that I had to have "something of my own." He made me responsible for the Foundation's international Nutrition Policy Program. It was a great boost for me to be put in charge of this program. The experience of someone I admire putting so much trust in me has impacted my own leadership style. In the following decades, I have often used this principle for motivating young professionals.

Communication was one of Lowell's greatest talents. It was an important instrument in his mentoring of many of us, no matter whether we were around him in the office or thousands of miles away. He was a master of asking critical questions and structuring ideas for solving them. He gave feedback on many issues and he solicited ideas from all corners. Even without today's digital technology, Lowell created an amazing network of professionals. Abe Weisblatt (formerly with the Agricultural Development Council and subsequently with Rutgers University) told me once that Lowell had built a "virtual department" for advancing the rural social sciences and agricultural technology in developing countries. I learned how important networks are, and I copied this approach successfully in my own work throughout the years.

A lot of his networking happened on the phone, but it was his writing of memos that impressed me most. He shared a lot of his drafts with me and gave me ample opportunity to uncover his strategies for good writing. I have never reached his level of excellence, but I certainly learned a lot. Another thing I learned from him was the preparation of meetings. His "trick" was to write down how he wanted the debate to proceed, then guide the meeting through the logic of his preparatory notes and, finally, simply modify his notes as minutes of the discussion.

During the years with Lowell in New York, I often felt that I was complementing my degrees from Austria and from Michigan State University with a degree from Purdue University and with a lot of Midwestern wisdom, some of it in solid academic terms, some through often funny but always apt metaphors like: "there are more ways to skin a cat" or "you cannot push on a string." There was his constant reminder that "we must grow two blades of grass where there was just one before." Some of these pieces of wisdom he had taken over from his own mentor, F.F. (Frosty) Hill, one of the founding fathers of the Green Revolution. Now famous is the directive to "find the key-log in the log jam" and build your strategy on the removal of the key-log. I often used these and similar words in conveying my own ideas.

Mentoring from a distance

After three years at the Foundation Headquarters, Lowell did what he had done with many others: He focused on my longer-term professional career. In a series of discussions, we developed a trajectory that would expose me to hands-on problems "in the field." Out of this dialog emerged two important assignments that gave me, as Lowell had predicted, a solid grounding in the practical aspects of development work. My first assignment was as the

Mary and Lowell Hardin.

Foundation's Program Advisor in North Africa with its hub in Tunisia. The second and even more challenging and rewarding one was the position as the Foundation's Program Advisor for West Africa and Sahel, based in Nigeria. In subsequent years, I have often copied Lowell's concern for my career with my own mentees.

Being "in the field" showed me the other side of Lowell's mentorship. There were memos. There were questions asked in letters. There were ideas conveyed in sharing notes and writings of others. There were also trips that brought Lowell to our projects. And there were invaluable summaries of his impressions about our work in the region and advice on what we might consider in the future. This too, I later applied as a leader and supervisor.

The personal aspects of mentoring

There were not only our programs, projects and grantees that were of interest to Lowell. He showed concern for our personal well-being and that of our families, and he was ably supported in this regard by his wife, Mary. She accompanied him on many of his missions and genuinely cared for our spouses and families.

After 10 years with the Ford Foundation and in a direct relationship to Lowell and his work, I decided to move on to new shores, but that did not end the close relationship with him. As someone said: "Once with him, you will always be one of Hardin's boys." This was also the case with me. I would keep him informed on what I was doing and would consult with him on issues where I was interested in his opinion and advice. And vice versa, he would share ideas that he thought would be important for me. In those exchanges there was always a mix of professional content and personal concern. A special treat were the Christmas letters that we received throughout all these years. They reached us in Tunisia, Nigeria, Austria, Germany, Italy, Bangladesh, and later in Washington, D.C.

Once a mentee, always a mentee

In 2000, Heidi and I returned to the U.S., and I developed the habit of calling Lowell quite regularly. From his questions about my work with the U.N. World Food Programme, I gathered that he continued to feel responsible for his mentorship role vis-à-vis myself. In our conversations, I often told him about what I had heard about other members of the "Hardin Network," and he would tell me about who had called him. Sometimes I exchanged mail or phone calls with former colleagues, and we would talk about Lowell's impact on our lives. As Don Winkelmann (former Director General of CIMMYT and former Chair of the CGIAR's Technical Advisory Committee) once summed it up: "Without Lowell's continuous mentoring throughout these many years, I could not have reached my potential and I would not have achieved what I did." I feel the same way.

Age and experience bring judgment and sometimes even wisdom. Dispense wisdom sparingly and only as required, like salt on your potatoes.

Roberto Lenton

Impressed by this gracious, decent, and unassuming man.

Roberto Lenton is Professor Emeritus of Biological Systems Engineering at the University of Nebraska–Lincoln. A specialist in water resources and sustainable development, he earned a civil engineering degree from the University of Buenos Aires and M.S. and Ph.D. degrees in hydrology and water resources systems from Massachusetts Institute of Technology (MIT). After serving as Assistant Professor of Civil Engineering at MIT, he joined the Ford Foundation as Program Officer in 1977, initially in the New Delhi office and later at the Foundation's headquarters in New York. He was responsible for the Foundation's work as Implementing Agency for the establishment of what is now the International Water Management Institute.

In 1987, he was appointed as the Institute's Director General, and served in that capacity until 1994. He subsequently held several international leadership positions, including as director of the Sustainable Energy and Environment Division of the United Nations Development Program (UNDP) in New York, Chair of the Technical Committee of the Global Water Partnership, Chair of the Inspection Panel of the World Bank, and (most recently) Founding Executive Director of the Daugherty Water for Food Global Institute at the University of Nebraska.

I first met Lowell in June 1977 when I was being interviewed at the Ford Foundation in New York for a position in New Delhi. It was my first visit to the Foundation's magnificent offices on 43rd Street, and a full day of meetings had been arranged for me. As luck would have it, my first meeting was with Lowell and two young colleagues, Werner Kiene and Joe Remenyi. At the time, I wasn't really quite sure who Lowell was, and it was only later that I realized I had met the great Lowell Hardin himself! I can't remember the details of the meeting nor what we talked about, but I do remember being impressed by this gracious, decent and unassuming man, who was clearly the boss yet quite willing to let his younger colleagues do much of the talking. I came away from this meeting and the others that followed with a clear sense that this was an organization and a group of people I very much wanted to join. The feeling must have been mutual, because shortly afterwards I was offered the position, and by August my family and I had arrived in India.

Even though he was based far away in New York, Lowell had a big impact on all of us in the Delhi office. References to "Uncle Lowell" came up constantly in meetings of our small agriculture and natural resources group, especially since our boss, Norman Collins, had worked closely with Lowell in New York before coming to Delhi and admired him greatly. Lowell also made periodic visits to India, which provided excellent opportunities to interact firsthand and get to know him.

But perhaps Lowell's greatest impact on our work came through the key role he played behind the scenes in the creation of what is now the International Water Management Institute, which became an important initiative of the Foundation in the late 1970s—and a major part of my life from then on. At that time, the CGIAR's Technical Advisory Committee had begun a serious effort to explore whether and how the CGIAR should tackle the issue of water management. Lowell, who had earlier been hugely instrumental in the creation of IRRI and CIAT and viewed the Foundation as a catalytic organization "that starts things and helps them get to the place where they can grow," as he once put it, was in a key position to help move this initiative forward—working in tandem with our agriculture and natural resources team in New Delhi, which had developed clear views on what kind of institute was needed. Undoubtedly as a result of Lowell's guidance, the TAC invited the Ford Foundation to join a small working group to review and further develop a proposal for an international research center on irrigation that had recently been commissioned. The conclusions of this working group, in turn, led to a meeting of interested donors and, further down the line, after Lowell had returned to Purdue, a decision to establish a new water management institute and ask the Foundation to act as Implementing Agency. When I moved to the Foundation's New York office, I became responsible for this implementation work, and subsequently left the Foundation to join the Institute as its second Director General.

Fortunately, that was not the end of my interactions with Lowell. After nine years at IWMI, I joined UNDP and represented UNDP in its role as one of the three co-sponsors of the CGIAR. At the initiative of UNDP, the co-sponsors had at that time instituted the William Mashler Award to honor those who had played leading roles in the development and growth of the CGIAR, and one of our first decisions when I joined the group of co-sponsors was to name Lowell as a recipient of the new award. Lowell was thus invited to participate in the annual CGIAR Centers' Week in Washington and was clearly touched by the award and the well-deserved recognition that came with it.

On my side, I felt truly privileged to be able to play a small role in honoring Lowell in this way. And in the two decades that followed, I had the good fortune to interact with numerous people who had worked closely with Lowell and whose eyes inevitably lit up whenever we spoke of Lowell and his influence on our lives. Notably, these have included Werner Kiene, who was present when I first met Lowell and with whom I worked closely years later when he was Chair of the World Bank Inspection Panel, and Gebisa Ejeta, with whom I have had the pleasure of teaming up since joining the Board of Governors of IWMI last year.

If someone needs a shoulder to cry on, listen to them, empathize. If you can't help it, cry too.

Selçuk Özgediz

I did not expect any questions. Boy, was I wrong!

Selçuk Özgediz devoted close to 30 years of his career to the CGIAR, as Management Adviser at the CGIAR Secretariat and consultant at the World Bank, Washington, D.C. Prior to joining the Bank as an economist in 1979, he taught at Bogazici University in Istanbul. In addition to the World Bank, he served as consultant to the European Union, FAO, OECD, USDA and other organizations. He is a graduate of Middle East Technical University in Ankara, Turkey (B.Sc., Economics and Statistics, 1966) and Michigan State University (M.S., Mathematical Statistics, 1968; M.A., Political Science, 1971; Ph.D., Political Science, 1976.) He has published in the areas of education policy, child development, organization development and governance. His latest publication was an institutional history of the CGIAR (The CGIAR at 40—Institutional Evolution of the World's Premier Agricultural Research Network, 2012).

It was my first CGIAR board meeting. I had just been appointed Management Adviser at the CGIAR Secretariat (a brand-new position), following a year working on the World Bank's annual World Development Report, 1983 that focused on the "Management in Development" theme. I introduced myself to the board, explained what my job entailed, told them I had to learn fast about the CGIAR and that I looked forward to having a good working relationship with the board and management of IFPRI. As this was just an introduction, I did not expect any questions.

Boy, was I wrong! I heard someone in a serious, loud voice: "Sir, what would you advise the CGIAR to do to reduce the impact of restricted contributions on the quality of science at the centers?" The speaker was a silver-haired, lean—and at the time I thought mean-looking—board member named Lowell Hardin. I did my best to answer his question with my limited knowledge of

CGIAR finances. I also decided then and there that I had to seek out people like this silver-haired fellow to better understand the dynamics of the CGIAR.

Upon returning to the Secretariat I asked my boss, Curt Farrar, who this fellow Lowell Hardin was. Curt explained the role Lowell had played in the founding of the CGIAR and the centers. He also mentioned that I should familiarize myself with a recent report Lowell had prepared, on behalf of a CGIAR panel, on The Role, Relationships and Responsibilities of Trustees of International Agricultural Research Centers. After reading it quickly I decided that I should reach out to Lowell and two members of that CGIAR panel (Omond Solandt and Louis Crouch) to get them interested in chairing some of the initial external management reviews of centers. Fortunately, all three were willing and eager to contribute, helping us kick-start the reviews in the 1980s. Solandt led the first reviews of CIP and CIAT, Crouch chaired the first IITA and ICRISAT reviews, and Lowell led the panels reviewing ILCA and IRRI. I worked with them on behalf of the CGIAR Secretariat.

Thus began my association with Lowell, which continued throughout his life. Lowell was invited to chair these and similar panels not because of his particular expertise in management, but for the quality of his judgment and his deep understanding of the unique conditions the centers operated in. He knew firsthand the rationale for creating the centers and (as an agriculture scientist) the nature of the science they practiced. I quickly discovered that he also knew how to balance his deep affection for the centers with the impartiality required to conduct an independent evaluation. Regardless of his personal relationship with a board member or center director, as a reviewer he made sure to keep his distance when conducting business.

Lowell helped me in understanding and deciphering the complexity of the CGIAR. The timing of the start of our relationship was perfect. He had just ended a long career looking at the CGIAR from a founding donor angle (the Ford Foundation) when I was in search of mentors at the start of my career in the CGIAR. We would spend endless hours discussing the origins of the centers, the personalities and rivalries involved, negotiations with host countries, the role of the World Bank, etc. I would pepper him with questions and he would ask me about recent thinking on organization development and corporate governance. He would call me "professor" and insist that I call him "Lowell."

In addition to our conversations about the CGIAR I benefited from observing his handling of people in contentious meetings. He was a good listener, always showing respect to the other party, never interrupting, and maintaining his formal stance. The situation was different in private, one-on-one settings, where he would use a softer approach in seeking a solution to a problem.

Lowell had well-honed skills in the use of the English language. The panels we were on invariably included people with different writing abilities and styles. Yet their collective report had to have linguistic uniformity in communicating the findings. Lowell was always ready with pen in hand to make things right. People rarely objected to the changes he had made.

His seminars at Purdue were legendary. Once he invited me to talk about strategic planning, which had gained prominence in the corporate world in the late 1980s and was being emulated in the public and nonprofit sectors. I had conducted strategic planning workshops at a few centers, starting with CIMMYT. I talked at his seminar and gave a short briefing to Bob Thompson and his colleagues on strategic planning and our experiences with management reviews of centers. A week after I returned to Washington, D.C., a package arrived in the mail. It was a Purdue blanket, with a nice thank-you note from Lowell.

Lowell was super careful to do things right. When we returned from an overseas trip he would head directly to the "agriculture" line at customs. He would hand to the inspectors a bag containing the shoes he had worn in fields overseas. He did not want to be the one bringing a foreign organism into U.S. soil.

While the primary focus of the management reviews was on the center as an institution and its board, Lowell had a keen interest in the well-being of the people who made up the center community, in particular the spouses and the children. He would meet with the spouses to listen to their concerns and invite confidential communication, if needed. Improvement suggestions of a general nature would be covered in the report. He would treat private, confidential cases (such as spousal abuse) discreetly, without naming individuals, in his communications with the management or the board.

When we finished the first external management review of IRRI in 1987, the IRRI and CGIAR communities were impressed with the report and its recommendations. He called me after the dust had settled to tell me that IRRI had offered him a seat on its board. "What was your answer?" I asked him. He replied: "I told them they should instead offer the seat to a younger person, as I am approaching 70. A younger person can contribute to IRRI many more years than I can beyond the six-year board term." At that time Lowell was still in his prime, and he continued to contribute effectively to the CGIAR and other organizations many more years.

I am grateful that fate brought Lowell and I together at the right stage in my career. He was a role model and mentor to me, as he was to many others. Our partnership enriched my career. More important, I admired and was influenced by the personal qualities he exhibited: humility, selflessness, respect for others, and caring for all human beings.

I will always remember you fondly, Uncle Lowell!

When you have worked together with others in some successful enterprise that required a team, don't shoulder your way forward to grab credit. Rather, step back to the side, out of the limelight.

Eugene Terry

At a time when self-confidence was not
my most obvious characteristic.

*Eugene Terry was born in Sierra Leone and received his higher education
in Canada: B.Sc. Agriculture and M.Sc. Plant Pathology from McGill University, and Doctorate in Plant Pathology from the University of Illinois,
Urbana-Champaign. Eugene has held senior research and institutional
leadership positions in regional and international institutions—first at
the International Institute of Tropical Agriculture (IITA) in Nigeria as
Plant Pathologist and later Director of International Programs; at the
West Africa Rice Development Association (WARDA, now AfricaRice)
as Director General, 1987–1996; as Crops Advisor to the Director of Agriculture and Rural Development, The World Bank, 1996–2002; and as
the Founding Director of the African Agricultural Technology Foundation (AATF), Nairobi, 2002–2004.*

*Eugene has served on the Boards of Trustees of the World Agro-Forestry
Centre (WAC-ICRAF, the World Vegetable Centre (WVC-AVRDC) and
now chairs the Advisory Board of the West Africa Centre for Crop Improvement (WACCI), hosted by the University of Ghana in Accra. Eugene
was awarded the Presidential (Mali Government) Award for Outstanding Contribution to Rice Science in Africa, and the Macdonald College/
McGill University Distinguished Alumni 2012 Award.*

I first met Lowell during his Ford Foundation tenure (1965–1982) when,
in his capacity as a senior agriculturist, he was engaged with other key
thinkers in laying the foundation for the global network of agricultural
research centers. That first encounter had taken place sometime around 1973–
74 during my first year as a newly hired plant pathologist at the International
Institute of Tropical Agriculture (IITA) in Ibadan, Nigeria. IITA, of course,

was one of the first international centers of the Consultative Group of International Agricultural Research (CGIAR) Network of research institutes worldwide. These CGIAR centers were created to address a broad range of issues in agriculture, fisheries, forestry, livestock, water and other natural resources management.

Lowell, as one of the pioneers of this innovative global concept, became an active participant and an observer at the meetings of the Board of Trustees of these centers. During these meetings, Lowell would often seek out Center scientists for one-on-one conversations to get a feel for the progress, opportunities and challenges resulting from the center's activities. I had just been hired as a junior scientist from the Faculty of Agriculture, Njala University College, and University of Sierra Leone. I must confess that, at the time, I was a little "green" and rather unsure of my "footing" in that "big bad world" of international agricultural research. Lowell must have quickly sensed how nervous and insecure I was feeling at the time. He had casually engaged me in conversation around the coffee table during one of the many coffee/tea breaks, and before I realized it, I was describing my vision for a Cassava Pathology Program at IITA. Lowell was in fact asking me to describe how the program I was hired to develop would serve the needs of the diverse constituents that made up the Cassava National Programs in Sub-Saharan Africa. Here we were—me, the green and insecure young scientist having been only just recently "initiated" into the hallowed corridors of international agricultural research, confronting the task to articulate what I considered a weighty subject to a "famous" and distinguished senior executive from the globally recognized Ford Foundation. It was with no small feeling of trepidation that I ventured to respond to Lowell's many questions.

Slowly, but assuredly, that admirable quality for which Lowell is now so well known, "putting people at ease," helped me relax. I found myself quite easily and comfortably talking at length about my work. I described for Lowell what I understood to be the major root and tuber crops' disease challenges, and the options and opportunities for their control. I was surprised, although in hindsight I should not have been, to find out that Lowell was already quite knowledgeable about some of the details of these challenges.

That first encounter, and my subsequent exchanges with this kind and gentle scholar, were among some of my most memorable experiences in dealing with those whom I regarded as among the venerable and influential pioneers of international agricultural research. I was impressed first and foremost with Lowell's ability to put people at ease, and at such a high comfort level, for them to so willingly share their thoughts and ideas with him without hesitation. Lowell's capacity for empathy and understanding was particularly appreciated by this insecure junior scientist, at a time in my career when self-confidence was not my most obvious characteristic.

Later, in my encounters with friends, colleagues, and past students of Lowell's, I confirmed what I had initially personally experienced—that I was not the only one who had been the beneficiary and recipient of the generosity of the spirit of this kind man. Much as I would have liked to think that I had been uniquely selected to enjoy this special treatment and attention, I soon discovered that Lowell was an equal opportunity dispenser of kindness, understanding, and generous professional support to all those whose paths had crossed his own path. I join those many other grateful recipients in honoring the memory of this great and kind human being.

People sometimes need someone to listen to them with a sympathetic ear, need to talk about what's on their mind. They need caring company, not advice. Just listen.

PART 2

Purdue University

Jay Akridge

What a terrific deal for a Dean.

Jay Akridge serves as Provost and Executive Vice President for Academic Affairs and Diversity at Purdue University. Previously, he served for nearly 10 years as the Glenn W. Sample Dean of the College of Agriculture at Purdue. An agricultural economist, he has spent his entire professional career at Purdue, earning both his M.S. and Ph.D. degrees there and then serving as a faculty member in the Department of Agricultural Economics for more than 20 years. An award-winning teacher, Jay has developed and led professional development programs with food and agribusiness managers in the U.S. and around the world. His research focuses on the marketing and managerial issues of agribusiness firms and technology adoption and buying behaviors of commercial farmers.

I knew of Dr. Lowell Hardin for many years before I truly knew him. For anyone in agricultural economics at Purdue, it was impossible not to know who Lowell was. As a graduate student and then a new faculty member, I regularly heard stories and news about his international work, his time with the Ford Foundation, the role he played in elevating international activity at Purdue. But it was my appointment as Dean of the College of Agriculture that provided me with the opportunity to get to work with him much more closely.

At that point, in the spring of 2008, Lowell was long retired but still very active in International Programs in Agriculture (IPIA) and still coming into work on a regular basis. What a terrific deal for a Dean: to have a person with Lowell's vast experience and insight as part of our leadership team, that we didn't have to pay! We joked about his "compensation"—and his tiny "office"—frequently.

Something that impressed me about Lowell early on was just how many of the people that I had much respect for in the international arena were deeply connected to Lowell: Gebisa Ejeta, Tom Hertel, Jess Lowenberg-DeBoer, Larry Murdock, to name some of the most prominent. These were professionals who were making a difference on global problems, people I was learning from and being mentored by, who were learning from and being mentored by Lowell. These were colleagues, mentors, and friends—relationships that I valued at the highest level—and Lowell was such an important part of each of their lives.

But, moving through my tenure as Dean, I soon found my own opportunities to experience and benefit from Lowell's wisdom and his insight. Over time, we had a number of important conversations that helped me think through some challenging issues and questions about our international programs and the direction we should be moving. To be direct: Lowell was one of the most thoughtful, insightful people I have ever interacted with. He thought deeply about, and brought so much experience to, any question I had for him. I believe this thoughtful nature, the fact that he took our conversations that seriously, was reflective of the fact that Lowell cared. He cared deeply about Purdue, he cared deeply about those working on international issues, he cared deeply about the state of the people of our world—and it showed in everything he did, in the relationships he developed. The interactions I had with him helped me truly understand why Lowell was so important to so many.

I am confident I do not have the words to fully characterize what Lowell meant to me, meant to Purdue Agriculture, to Purdue University, and frankly, to the world. There is no doubt in my mind that Lowell's expansive vision, his passion for international work, his global perspective, his relentless drive to make a difference, his caring nature, and his mentorship of the next generation of leaders brought a global perspective to all we do as a College of Agriculture. Lowell's legacy at Purdue is the fact that we look at global research and engagement, and international education, as a fundamental part of who we are as a College of Agriculture. We can't thank Lowell enough for his role in launching us on this global journey. Helping us understand how to put the power of the land-grant model to work in building a better world was Lowell's gift to us all.

*N*ever say "Do this!" or "Do that!" to the person you are trying to help. You are a guide, not a commander. Rather, roll out your best thought, not as a single assertion, but as one of possible actions, each examined on its merits and downsides, without bias. The person before you must decide.

Tom Campbell

They say that only about the great ones.

Tom Campbell is the photographer for the Purdue University College of Agriculture. From 1997 to 2016, he was the managing editor of Connections, the alumni publication for the college. Campbell earned a bachelor's degree in radio and television from Purdue University in 1978.

With Lowell Hardin on your side, nothing was out of reach. Lowell Hardin was already a certified legend in agriculture before I started my career in the College of Agriculture in 1997.

To me he was the guy who wore the perfect Orville Redenbacher costume every day, and not just on Halloween. He worked down in the basement of the Ag Administration building. I was up on the second floor. And though the building wasn't that big, we didn't cross paths all that often.

It took me a while to find the true measure of this incredible man. In fact, I got to know him best through the deep friendships he established with three faculty members, Larry Murdock, Gebisa Ejeta and Tom Hertel. Those friendships were shared with me when I was asked to put together a story on Lowell's passing in 2015 at the age of 97.

Hardin deeply and profoundly impacted the lives and careers of these men and certainly others within the College of Agriculture. But these three had a special bond with Hardin. They called him friend, advisor, mentor, and, perhaps the highest praise of all, father.

The common thread shared by Murdock, Ejeta and Hertel is that all three are committed to solving the problems of global food security and world hunger. All three are dedicated to continuing the legacy of visionaries like Hardin and Nobel Peace Prize laureate Norman Borlaug, who saw a need to develop the field of international agriculture half a century ago.

Anybody working on that agenda always had Hardin's ear. But these three had Hardin's heart, too.

When Hardin passed away in 2015, Murdock was in Burkina Faso, Africa, spreading the good work of PICS (Purdue Improved Crop Storage) to thousands of farmers, many of whom just want to feed their family enough food to get to tomorrow.

Murdock, Purdue's distinguished professor of entomology, wanted to shorten his 10-day trip to fly 7,000 miles home to pay tribute to his old friend, mentor and life coach.

But Hardin wouldn't have wanted that. And Murdock knew it.

So he spent some time in thought, reliving memories of Hardin. Larry and Susie Murdock grieved for their loss. For everyone's loss. Then he composed this letter to Lowell's three children.

> I am saddened not only by the loss of your wonderful dad—and of my best friend and mentor—but by the mean turn of fate that caused me to be thousands of miles away, in Burkina Faso, and so prevented me from attending his memorial service.
>
> My only solace is knowing that Lowell would understand, and say something to the effect that I "had more important things to do." My only rejoinder would be to remind him that were it not for him and his urging 30 years ago, I would not be where I am as I write—in a faraway place. I likely would never have done international development work at all.
>
> I'm sorry, too, that I shall not be able to visit Lowell when I return and share with him the adventures of the last 10 days in Burkina. I won't be able to tell him there were some 10,000 people in attendance at a ceremony held yesterday in a dusty village in the northwest part of the country, a village with no paved roads, the nearest asphalt being 50 bone-jarring miles away.
>
> I won't be able to tell him about the dancing and singing and colorful, smiling people and the major prizes (push carts, bicycles, cooking stoves and more) for those women who used PICS bags most effectively in a public competition. It was thrilling, and the story would have thrilled Lowell.
>
> He won't be there to ply me with questions, and I won't be able to tell him that on the ride back to Ouagadougou, we finally hit a paved road. Alongside that highway there was a large sign: "This

highway was built by financial help of the American people." Low-ell would have been proud, as I was.

It was Hardin who introduced Murdock to international agriculture when he retired—yes, retired—from the Ford Foundation and returned to Purdue in 1982. He opened the door for Murdock to go to Kenya to review a major insect physiology project, Murdock's first trip to Africa. Murdock has made some 60 trips to Africa as a researcher. After each of those trips, he would seek out Hardin for a debriefing and perhaps a blessing. Murdock always wanted to know if Hardin thought his research was staying the course.

"He had a way of telling you truths that you may not have wanted to hear," Murdock said. "But Lowell could do it in a way that made it sound like a positive thing. That was one of his gifts."

It was a gift he freely shared.

"All that we have done as a college in international agriculture came out of Lowell's deep interest in what was going on around the world," Murdock said. "He genuinely cared about people."

Hertel, a distinguished professor of agricultural economics, was working for the Ford Foundation in Botswana when Hardin interviewed him for a position at the foundation's headquarters in New York City.

Hardin hired Hertel as an assistant program officer. They were close friends the remainder of Hardin's life.

"He was with me all of my professional career, going back to when I was barely out of my teenage years, trying to figure out life. But we had this deeper personal connection," Hertel said. "He was a part of our family. He was always my lifelong mentor—he mentored everyone—but for me, it was always about family first."

"Lowell and Mary became our parents," said Hertel. "They were an integral part of our wedding."

Lowell was the photographer, and Mary scurried about the Hertel home making sure all in attendance signed their guest book. In the years to come, Lowell and Mary would become the grandparents to the Hertel children.

As an advisor and mentor, Hertel said, Hardin's greatest strength was that he never really offered advice.

Gebisa and Lowell Hardin in a sorghum research field at the Purdue
University Ag Center for Research and Education (ACRE) in 2009.

"The great thing about all mentors—and Lowell was the best—is they never
tell you what to do. They listen, summarize, then they ask a couple of questions. At the end, you then realize what the right decision is."

At Hardin's memorial service, Hertel eulogized, "With Lowell as your
cheerleader, nothing seemed out of reach."

Gebisa Ejeta said his frequent discussions with Hardin were like "getting
a degree from the University of Lowell Hardin."

"If I were on campus, I can't recall a week going by without seeing Lowell," said the 2009 World Food Prize laureate and distinguished professor
of agronomy.

"We had nothing in common. He was an economist, and I was a plant
scientist."

Hardin grew up in a Quaker family on a small Indiana farm in Henry
County in the days following World War I. Ejeta was raised in a small village in
the rolling hills of Ethiopia. Yet they shared a bond few people ever experience.

"I was enthralled with the things I would hear from him, and he liked what
I had to tell him about everywhere that I went. I look back at that experience

and realize what an incredible education that was for me," Ejeta said. "It was a chance to grow as a person and as a professional."

When Gebisa was named the recipient of the World Food Prize, no one took more delight in the honor than Hardin, who helped pen Ejeta's nominating letter.

"For those he loved," Ejeta said, "he spoke with an uncharacteristic lack of reservation."

And it continued to Lowell Hardin's last days. As Hardin's health was declining, Ejeta would visit every day, checking on his old friend. "We had an uncommon relationship," Ejeta said. "It was based, quite simply, on pure human love. When you look at the generational difference, the background difference, there is nothing we had in common, other than this service that we were both committed to. I guess that was the common denominator. Then we built a human relationship on top of that. He would call me one of his sons. And I would call him my father."

Lowell Hardin's life spread across 10 decades. It is difficult to imagine living that long and that well. And still it could be said that Lowell died much too soon. They say that only about the great ones.

But that was Lowell Hardin.

The best form of caring is listening. Helping others starts with it.

Tom Hertel

For the first time I was able truly to reciprocate.

Tom Hertel grew up in Ithaca, New York, in a family of Cornellians. In an effort to put some distance between himself and this dominant legacy, he studied in Germany, North Carolina and New Jersey, as well as working overseas and for the Ford Foundation in New York City, before returning to Cornell for a Ph.D. in Agricultural and Applied Economics. Upon completing that degree in 1983, he took a job at Purdue University, where he has been employed ever since, rising through the ranks from Assistant to Associate, to Full and then to Distinguished Professor of Agricultural Economics. He has served as major advisor for more than 40 Ph.D. students.

In 1992, he founded the Global Trade Analysis Project (GTAP) which now comprises more than 19,000 individuals in 175 countries. GTAP facilitates economy-wide analysis of trade, environment and agricultural policies. Dr. Hertel's most recent work has been of an interdisciplinary nature and focuses on climate change and sustainability. In recognition of this work, in 2013 he became the first recipient of Purdue's Research and Scholarship Distinction Award.

I arrived at the Ford Foundation offices to interview for the position of Assistant Program Officer in International Agriculture, having resigned in disgust from a Dutch development consulting firm; I was "on the rebound." Up to that point, I had been absolutely convinced that I would not become an academic or an ivory tower person, but rather I would work in the international development field and have a direct impact on people's lives. I got in the door for this interview on the basis of my prior work for the Ford Foundation in Botswana. I had produced a report on the impact of what we now call "globalization" on low-income households in rural Botswana. It was a terrific experience and caught the attention of Lowell through his East Africa Program Lead—John Gerhart.

It wasn't long into our interview that Lowell figured out our mutual connection to George Warren—my grandfather, and a mentor of Lowell at Cornell. From that point on, it was likely a done deal. Lowell had lost his previous assistant, Joe Reminyi, when he returned to Australia and was in need of filling this slot. So I lucked out and was hired!

Lowell had a knack for mentoring his assistants. I was immediately folded into what we would now call his "workflow." This entailed extensive correspondence with his global network of individuals working around the world in international agriculture. His special passion at the time was to insert social scientists into the international agricultural research centers to ensure that the new technologies being developed were economically profitable and socially productive. All of this correspondence was typed in duplicate, with the original being mailed off and the duplicate crossing my desk and then going into the "chron file," where detailed records of all of Lowell's correspondence resided. When coupled with his pocket-size notebooks in which he recorded his observations, names and other notes during his travels, this was a powerful system to connect people, ideas and institutions around the world.

I was always impressed with the way Lowell combined personal and professional interests. He never failed to keep tabs on the families of his mentees, and he and Mary often hosted these individuals and families when they visited New York. Mary and I developed a close relationship during my year in New York, as she took me under her wing.

Despite Lowell's mentoring, the Ford Foundation was not a good fit for me. At that point I had tried the private sector and the foundation sector, but in both cases it was clear to me I needed a set of skills I did not possess at that time. Lowell saw that and undertook the challenging task of convincing me to go back for a Ph.D.—something that I had adamantly resisted, having come from a family already full of academics. As he did with all his mentees, Lowell kept me in his sights during this time. Indeed, three years later, when I was on the job market and contemplating a move to Massachusetts, I got a call from Lowell, who had recently returned to Purdue. He said "Tom, did you

Tom Hertel and Lowell Hardin.

know that Purdue has an opening?" As I learned later, he simultaneously put in a call to the Department Head at Purdue, Paul Farris, saying, "Paul, have you considered Tom Hertel for your position at Purdue?" The rest is history! Lowell was a born matchmaker!

Upon moving to West Lafayette, I renewed and deepened my friendship with Lowell and Mary, and they effectively became grandparents for our children as well as embracing my wife, Adriela Fernandez. Lowell was even the photographer at our wedding! We celebrated Thanksgiving and birthdays together, and Lowell would also drop in to my office to "see how things were going." When I started the GTAP effort, Lowell was there to advise me on how to set up a robust governance structure. The consortium which we established—based on Lowell's guiding principles from years of working with the international centers—is still functioning 25 years later!

A turning point in our relationship came about when Lowell and Mary had a severe auto accident. Mary was badly injured and Lowell suffered emotionally, blaming himself for the accident. For the first time I was able truly to reciprocate, listening to Lowell and providing him with support. This was the first time he shared his deeper feelings, and it was after this time that our relationship moved onto a peer footing.

There are a few other moments that really stand out in my memories of Lowell. One of those took place in our family room when I was playing with Sarah, and Lowell remarked that he was glad I was spending lots of time with the kids. In his time things were different, he said. He was extremely busy as Department Head, and the division of labor between Lowell and Mary was such that he spent relatively little time with his young children. If he could have reached back and changed his personal history in that moment, he would eagerly have done so.

Another important moment for both Lowell and me occurred in 2010 when I was preparing my address to the Agricultural and Applied Economics Association (AAEA). Lowell's communication tips were invaluable in making this talk more accessible. And, as an aside, he pointed out to me that he, himself, had given the Presidential Address to this association nearly five decades before! Furthermore, my grandfather—and Lowell's mentor—George Warren, had given the address a century before me! I built this into my talk, and it was the first time I had publicly acknowledged this kinship with George Warren—a founder of our profession, but a personality too imposing for me to deal with up to that point.

Lowell and I "shared" birthdays: November 16 and 17, and we often celebrated together. On the occasion of his 95th birthday, I wrote the following, which I later delivered at his memorial service.

The seven ages of Lowell Hardin
Presented by Tom Hertel, with apologies to
William Shakespeare, May 2, 2015

All the world's a stage, and all the men and women merely players;
They have their entrances and their exits, and Lowell Hardin played many parts.
His acts being in seven ages.

At first the Midwestern farm boy, fresh and naïve, raised by a stern but loving father and a nurturing mother in a small, close-knit Indiana community. Growing up during the Depression, schooling, farm work, 4-H livestock judging competitions, elocution lessons, and trapping skunks filled his every waking moment!

Then it was off to Purdue for a second age filled with education and broadening experiences. AGR house provided a home away from home. And editorial work at the Exponent sharpened Lowell's pen. This also led him to fellow editor Mary Cooley and a memorable first date on "Tobacco Road"! Lowell, on his knees before Mary, decorated the pages of the Purdue Exponent student newspaper on April 1st!

Lowell's third age, and his career as an agricultural economist, was launched by Doc Young—who guided this bright young man to graduate school, high above Cayuga's waters, at Cornell. There, with the support of his beautiful new bride, Mary, Lowell survived the language requirement by the skin of his teeth (thanks largely to Mary's facility with German!) and thrived under the tutelage of Warren, Pearson, Reed and Frosty Hill.

Lowell's fourth age was that of Purdue Professor. What started off with studies of farm work simplification evolved into a career in international affairs. First came his assignment in Japan—part of the postwar reconstruction effort. Then came his role in launching the Agricultural Economics component of the Purdue-Vicosa Project with Brazil, an effort that transformed a sleepy country college into a major international research university. This was also the age of child-rearing, with Tom, Joy and Peter (the "bonus baby") arriving in close succession and blossoming under Mary and Lowell's loving parenting.

This leads into Lowell's fifth age, that of international agriculturalist at the Ford Foundation. Together with Mary, the two brought a healthy dose of Midwestern sensibility and hospitality to the Big Apple. The success of the International Agricultural Research Centers, and the ensuing Green Revolutions in Asia and Latin America during this period, owes much to the quality of the individuals involved in the Centers. Lowell and Mary nurtured this network, both at home and on the road. From his office on East 43rd Street in NYC, Lowell invented the world's first "virtual network" of individuals working around the globe on common issues—bound together through Lowell's diligent correspondence, phone calls, and periodic visits. Introducing social scientists into these laboratory-heavy research institutions was one of Lowell's critical contributions to the CGIAR centers. His sage advice altered the professional trajectories of many, many individuals who went on to successful and rewarding careers. One of those was a 24-year-old would-be internationalist who was struggling to find his way in the world. Lowell gave me a chance to work for him as Assistant Program Officer, during which time all of his correspondence passed across my desk. Via this process of osmosis, I learned how to cultivate an international network of individuals seeking to achieve a broader vision. These were skills which I was able to bring to bear nearly two decades later when I reached the appropriate point in my own career.

Lowell's sixth age brought him back to Purdue once more—at the siren call of that insistent mistress, the Wabash River! Between hosting a lively interdisciplinary seminar series on food security and mentoring a new generation of Purdue internationalists, Lowell began yet another meaningful, impactful career. Taking his greatest joy in the accomplishments of others, he watched as his mentees—Gebisa Ejeta, Larry Murdock, myself, and many of those here today—strive to make contributions to international development. With Lowell as your cheerleader, there was nothing that seemed out of reach.

In his seventh age, Lowell played the role of loving caregiver, along with his continuing and ever more important roles as father, grandfather, mentor and friend. The collection of diverse friends and colleagues who visited him over this period, seeking advice, encouragement and someone to really listen to them, offers ample testament to the vitality of Lowell's seventh age—and indeed his entire life.

We are happy that Lowell is once again reunited with Mary. Together they make a fantastic team, and they will no doubt keep an eye out for all of us mortals as we attempt to live up to their hopes and expectations. They will both live on in all of our own acts of kindness and humanity—especially the small, unexpected and deeply thoughtful gestures of support for our fellow travelers.

When someone comes back from a work-related trip or meeting, ask them what they learned, what they felt, did, or thought. Share the adventure.

Katy Ibrahim

You also knew he had no time for fools.

Katy Ghawi Ibrahim was born in Jerusalem, Palestine, and educated in a French-speaking school where she also studied Arabic and English. After receiving her baccalaureate degree, she came to the U.S. on a student visa to attend a private girls' high school to improve her English. She remained in the U.S. to further her education. After graduating from Downer College of Lawrence University in Appleton, Wisconsin, she returned to Jerusalem for several years before immigrating to the U.S.

Katy's career at Purdue spanned 32 years, during which she managed projects in the International Programs in Agriculture (IPIA) office led by Dr. D. Woods Thomas, Director. In the early '80s, Dr. Thomas shared that Dr. Lowell Hardin would be joining the office to manage a USDA-funded Program Support Grant. Dr. Hardin's office was next to Katy's, which meant that the two of them were in almost daily contact. She assisted Dr. Hardin to organize on-campus international seminars. She also supported his recruiting of young faculty to become involved in international research and development activities.

This is probably one of the most difficult writing tasks I have done in a long time, namely describing my relationship with Dr. Hardin. There are so many memories and experiences we've had, I hardly know where to begin. Certainly, he brought a unique perspective to international projects and, in my opinion, many of our faculty (too many to mention) who have succeeded professionally in that arena owe a great deal to Dr. Hardin's mentoring. The College of Agriculture's impact and importance in international research likewise owes much to Dr. Hardin.

I first met Dr. Hardin when he returned to campus in the early '80s. I didn't know much about him except for the fact that he had been instrumental in setting up several international research centers worldwide. Little did I realize that he would become my mentor in handling the many intricacies of international work I was involved in, and that he would also become a wonderful friend.

In my opinion, he was a real "Renaissance" man, with so much insight and knowledge that you never left his office without learning something new, feeling good about yourself and knowing that he would tell you the facts as they were, regardless of your position on the matter. You also knew he had no time for fools.

I benefited so much from knowing and working with him in different activities he planned through our office: international seminars, involving young faculty to work internationally and covering their travel under the Title XII funding he had secured from Washington. One of those was Larry Murdock, who became fully committed to international research. Of course, Dr. Hardin asked me to assist in getting Larry to travel to Africa and he was soon "hooked." In his capacity as a wise mentor, Dr. Hardin was sought by many Ag faculty (too many to mention and many long gone) for advice, insight, assistance in making connections and using his unbelievable list of contacts and friends to help out.

On a personal note, I always sought him out when I was feeling frustrated about my work dealing with the problems of international research. He never failed me! After talking with Dr. Hardin, I always felt rejuvenated and ready to do my best. Of course, while in his office you always knew when you had used up your time. He had a pleasant way of ending a conversation without making you feel badly, and it always worked.

When Dr. Hardin retired and was not well, I asked several ladies in our office if they could help out. Trish Sipes, our computer expert, would go once a week to his apartment at Westminster retirement center and assist with computer "stuff." Lonni Kucik was lined up to go visit Lowell and she often took her daughter, Lizzie, along. I volunteered to do his food shopping on Saturdays and visit with him at that time. We even organized a birthday party at his apartment, and he was so grateful as to warm our hearts. On several occasions, I attended seminars he held at Westminster, and I ended up being not only the hostess but also meeting many of the retirees.

He was genuinely interested in my family and would always ask about them, and he shared the same about his children, whom I got to know, Tom, Joy and Peter.

In the late 1990s, Dr. Hardin sent me a personal note with a copy of his *Memoir of an International Farmer*. He wrote, "Please accept it as a token of our appreciation for your friendship and ever-willing support. We hold your exceptional array of talents in high esteem." I have read that note and others he sent me so many times, and would you believe that after all these years I can still envision him being here with me. What a wonderful man. I miss him!

Never speak unkindly of anyone. Ever. It's a matter of integrity and trust.

Laurie Kitch

After eventually exhausting myself, I finally
fell silent, somewhat apprehensive.

*Laurie Kitch received his M.S. and Ph.D. degrees in Plant Breeding and
Genetics from Purdue University (1982 and 1987, respectively). He began
his career as a plant breeder/agronomist at Purdue University as part
of the USAID Bean/Cowpea Collaborative Research Support Program
(CRSP) Purdue-Cameroon project headed by Distinguished Professor
Larry Murdock, spending the majority of his time in West Africa.*

*His research and development work focused on cowpea (Vigna unguic-
ulata) plant breeding, agronomy and pest management. He played an
important role in the development and release of high-yielding pest- and
disease-resistant cowpea cultivars and the development of cowpea storage
technologies, including the PICS (Purdue Improved Crop Storage) bags,
which have been disseminated globally.*

*Following his work at Purdue University, Dr. Kitch joined the FAO in
1998, serving as the Regional Plant Production and Protection Officer for
Southern and Eastern Africa, with responsibility for programming in 22
countries. Kitch provided project formulation, management and technical
oversight for several high-impact agricultural development projects and
served as the FAO focal point for biotechnology and biosafety in Africa.
Dr. Kitch went on to serve as the first Representative of the Food and Agriculture Organization of the United Nations (FAO) to the State of Qatar,
where he assisted the Qatar Government in planning and implementing
agriculture and food security policy and regulatory reform, and in developing various agricultural projects.*

*After retiring from FAO, he worked for the Government of Qatar for
several years as a Senior Advisor for their National Food Security Program. Dr. Kitch is currently the CEO of PICS Global Inc., a social enterprise established to commercialize the PICS technology across the globe.*

My first experience with Dr. Hardin was perhaps my most unforgettable. As I was about to begin a Ph.D. program, my major Professor, Dr. John Axtell, had proposed that I serve as a graduate student research assistant as part of the USAID-funded Niger Cereals Research and Extension Project involving the Government of Niger and Purdue University. After expressing my interest, it was proposed that I meet with Dr. Hardin for an interview. The interview took place in the somewhat intimidating main conference room in the Agricultural Administration Building.

After pleasantly introducing himself, Dr. Hardin, in a very relaxed manner, asked me to tell him "all about myself." He would like to know what I had done with my life up to this point. Although I did experience a somewhat panic-induced "my life flashed before my eyes" moment, the narrative I produced did not flash by. With his continuing display of true interest, I more confidently rambled on for at least a half hour but quite probably longer. With such an open-ended format, and seemingly captivated audience, I unfortunately found myself uncontrollably wandering through an excessive number of childhood and early adult anecdotes. However, after eventually exhausting myself, I finally fell silent, somewhat apprehensive, realizing that I had now just presented myself up for some type of verdict.

After a brief but pleasant moment of reflection, Dr. Hardin proceeded to summarize my entire life story for me in, I believe, something like five concise bullet points—requiring probably less than two minutes. He then inquired whether he had captured the essence. Despite my frantic efforts, I couldn't come up with a thing that he had missed. I was absolutely amazed. Yes, I did feel pretty stupid, but then again, I was only a graduate student. This was the conclusion of a life-changing lesson for me on how to "get to the point" in thinking and presenting. Even after a lifetime of practice, I have still not achieved what I consider to be the "gold standard" as set by Dr. Hardin. Truly a great mind and inspiring human being.

Never let your age or station in life get in the way of new experiences. Seize every opportunity you can, no matter your age. Age may need a cane, but even so it can be ready for a new adventure.

Lonni Kucik

He gave so much and asked for so little.

Lonni Kucik is a long-standing employee of Purdue University's Office of International Programs in Agriculture (IPIA). She started in IPIA in 2001 as a project assistant on the Integrated Pest Management Collaborative Research Support Program (IPM CRSP) and in 2002 became the Administrative Assistant for IPIA Director, David Sammons. In 2007, she and her husband, Dave, adopted Elizabeth-Marie "Lizzi" Qiulan from China. She decided to work part-time in IPIA, so transitioned back to work in the role of project assistant. During her 18 years in IPIA she assisted with projects in Afghanistan, Colombia, Guatemala, Honduras, Jordan, Kenya, Mali, and Senegal. She has planned visits for international visitors from Africa, Asia, Europe and Latin America. She really enjoys contributing to Purdue's international development and collaboration efforts. Her approach and understanding of working with international people have been greatly shaped by knowing Dr. Hardin.

Where to start my story about knowing and loving Dr. Lowell Hardin? When I started IPIA in 2001, Dr. Hardin was our Assistant Director at the age of 84. I learned quickly that he had a wealth of knowledge and was generous in sharing his insights and experiences. Since he and Mary had traveled to most parts of the world, he could add to any international research discussion and shared many interesting experiences, insights and anecdotes. I'm sorry to report that my memory fails me in recalling most of the details of his stories—but I'm reminded by the plaque that hung in IPIA for years, and now is housed in Purdue's Library Archive, of his time working in Aleppo, Syria, with ICARDA. He spoke so positively of the people and the country Syria—and his time working there with ICARDA. This plaque was created and presented to honor his service as Vice Chairman of ICARDA Board of Trustees from 1979 to 1985.

Through his role modeling, I learned from Dr. Hardin "you will catch more flies with sugar than vinegar" and "it's not work if you love what you're doing." He demonstrated these lessons every day. Over our 11 years working together in IPIA, we were often office mates. As an Emeritus Professor he kept regular office hours, attended all our IPIA staff meetings, and organized monthly International Agriculture Seminars with some AMAZING researchers. He gave so much and asked for so little in exchange. I remember one day he arrived to IPIA and told me he got a raise! I said, "Dr. Hardin, we don't pay you." He said, "I know, but the parking fees went up and I get my parking pass for free." He was a man who showed "joy" in the way he lived and approached life.

That joy was contagious throughout our office. We loved to celebrate each birthday with him. For his 97th birthday we brought a birthday lunch to his house and took photos to document the occasion.

However, there was one area in which his performance was questioned by staff—and that was his driving. He was careful, but his vision was compromised. I believe he had only one eye that was functional, and he had macular degeneration in that eye. He would periodically go in for a shot in his good eye to slow the disease progression. When we had an office lunch off campus,

Happy birthday lunch with his co-workers.

Birthday celebrators: Trish Sipes, Linda Vallade, Dr. Hardin,
Katy Ibrahim, Kara Hartman and myself.

NO ONE wanted to ride with Dr. Hardin. We usually persuaded him to join in a carpool with someone else driving.

Dr. Hardin loved it when our daughter Lizzi came for a visit. She sometimes brought him some "artwork" for his refrigerator. He always engaged her, usually had a small gift for her, like books his daughter-in-law Karen passed to him from her role as a children's book reviewer, or doll clothes Mary had made, and even shared his family's tradition of building apple Santas at Christmastime. He was the grandpa Lizzi never had, since both of her grandfathers had passed before she was born.

My family and I feel greatly blessed to have had Dr. Hardin as a very dear friend. I still have the photos shown here in my office, to help me remember to live by the lessons I learned from this very special man.

The best teaching is done by example. Your example.

Jess Lowenberg-Deboer

There will be other opportunities.

Professor James (Jess) Lowenberg-DeBoer currently holds the Elizabeth Creak Chair of Agri-Tech Applied Economics at Harper Adams University, Newport, Shropshire, United Kingdom. From 1985 to 2017, he was on the faculty at Purdue University. He started as assistant professor in the Department of Agricultural Economics and rose through the ranks to become Professor of Excellence of International Entrepreneurship in 2015.

From 1988 to 1992, he was the senior economist and team leader for the Niger Applied Agricultural Research Project (NAARP), a U.S. Agency for International Development (USAID) institutional building project in the Republic of Niger, West Africa. From 2004 to 2015, he was Associate Dean and Director of Purdue International Programs in Agriculture. Following his retirement from Purdue in 2017, he is Emeritus Professor of Excellence in International Entrepreneurship at Purdue.

I met Lowell Hardin when he interviewed at Purdue in 1984. We became better acquainted when I worked on the Purdue project in the Republic of Niger. We would meet at the IPIA office when I came back for campus debriefing. But I only came to know Lowell well when he became Associate Dean for IPIA in 2004. He had the title of "Assistant Director for International Programs in Agriculture" and so he jokingly called me his "boss." In reality he was the IPIA senior advisor. When there was a very tough problem in IPIA (e.g., personnel, navigating university politics, relationships with international institutions), I would seek his perspective. Because of his long experience at Purdue and in international agricultural research, Dr. Hardin could put problems in context.

For example, the International Institute for Tropical Agriculture (IITA) was one of IPIA's key research and development partners. Lowell was part of the Ford Foundation team that founded IITA. He pointed out that IITA (and the rest of the Consultative Group for International Agricultural Research, CGIAR) were created with an expected life of 25 years. Dr. Hardin and the other founders felt that in 25 years IITA should have solved the problems of African agriculture. He noted that unfortunately IITA did not work itself out of a job, but instead became a bureaucracy with a strong interest in institutional self-preservation.

Lowell was committed to public service through agricultural development, but he also cared deeply about the people who devoted their lives to agricultural research. He understood that international researchers and their families had to be supported and encouraged. When I was proposed for a leadership role in IITA, Lowell helped me prepare for the interview. He shared IITA review reports and board of directors' documents. We had several long discussions about the future of IITA. When I returned from the interview, having been passed over for the position, Lowell came to my office and told me a story about how on one occasion, when he had tried and failed for a position at the *Purdue Exponent*, the student newspaper, his mother told him that while the *Exponent* was a great opportunity, there will be other opportunities. In that context he told me: "Yes, there is only one IITA, but there will be other opportunities."

Lowell's example was crucial in my choice of opportunities after leaving Purdue administration. Dr. Hardin left the Ford Foundation in 1981 when they de-emphasized agriculture. He returned to West Lafayette and made the most of his role as emeritus professor. He played an active role in IPIA programs, he wrote and published, and traveled frequently to help guide CGIAR evaluations and strategy.

When I stepped down from my IPIA administrative role in 2015, I wanted to re-engage in research. An opportunity came in the form of an offer of an endowed professorship at Harper-Adams University, focused on thought leadership in the economics of agricultural technology. Following Lowell Hardin's example of late career productivity, I did not let the challenge of complex immigration rules, adapting to life in the United Kingdom, and learning to navigate British academia stand in my way.

Learn to speak, write and edit clearly. Good ideas are injured by poor expression.

Rabi Mohtar

I stopped by Lowell's office to consult about sabbatical options.

Rabi H. Mohtar, Dean, Faculty of Agricultural and Food Sciences (FAFS), the American University of Beirut, is also a TEES Research Professor in the Department of Biological and Agricultural Engineering and the Zachry Department of Civil Engineering at Texas A&M University. At A&M, Mohtar founded the Water-Energy-Food Nexus Initiative and serves as an Advisor to the Energy Institute. He is adjunct professor at Texas A&M–Qatar, and was founding executive director of the Qatar Environment and Energy Research Institute (QEERI), Qatar Foundation.

At Purdue University, Mohtar was the inaugural director of Purdue's Global Engineering Programs, and developed the concept of Global Design Teams: real-world, full-cycle design experiences that help raise global awareness; he continues his affiliation with Purdue as an adjunct professor. Mohtar is a Governor of the World Water Council, a Senior Non-Resident Fellow at OCP Policy Center, a Fellow of the American Society of Agricultural and Biological Engineers, and a Distinguished Alumnus of the American University of Beirut.

During the fall of 2002, following six years at Purdue and during regular visits to IPIA, I stopped by Lowell's office to consult about sabbatical options. I had been pursuing an intense academic track at Purdue and, beyond my Lebanese heritage, there was very little global in my professional portfolio. Lowell suggested I contact Michel Petit, then an agricultural economist at CIRAD in Montpellier, France. I did so, with the result that I went to Montpellier to work with CIRAD and IRD colleagues during my sabbatical of 2002–2003.

This experience opened the door wide for an internationally rich career for years to come. My French colleagues, with whom I co-developed the pedostructure concept, also helped put milestones in my career through insights that augmented my knowledge of soil and water and of the thermodynamics and chemistry of soils. It was thanks to the nurturing, kind, and most unassuming nature of Lowell that I followed his advice and benefited from an enriching and globally satisfying career.

Being a mentor is a two-way street. You do your best to counsel, encourage and share experience with young people. In return you get appreciation, stimulation and a feeling of usefulness.

Larry Murdock

Such was the remarkable loom of
memories between Lowell's ears.

*In the late 1970s, Larry became a Purdue Assistant Professor of Ento-
mology after six years of postdoctoral research and teaching in Europe
(Konstanz, Germany; Naples, Italy; and Plymouth, England) and at the
University of Wisconsin medical school. Thanks to Lowell, he was able
to make his first trip to Africa in 1985, where in Kenya he reviewed a
multimillion-dollar research project. This opened his eyes to the dire needs
of Africa. For example, he was shocked to encounter a college-educated
Kenyan who could only find employment throwing rocks into sorghum
research plots to scare away birds. Africa needed not only education, but
jobs. But Larry also saw big needs and opportunities for research in Africa.
He became intrigued by African cultures and by the idea that work in Africa offered a bit of adventure as well as some personal rewards.*

*In the course of time and after many talks and encouragement from
Lowell, in 1987 Larry launched a USAID-supported CRSP project involving Purdue and Cameroonian scientists. Its chief objective was to de-
vise novel but simple and economical ways for Cameroonian farmers to
safely store their cowpea grain after harvest. Cowpea (black-eyed pea) is
a key food in much of Africa. Better postharvest storage promised to make
more food available to Cameroonian farmers and consumers plus gen-
erate cash incomes for farmers from the sale of their excess grain. Larry's
USAID project lasted 15 years and led to the invention and development of
the Purdue Improved Crop Storage (PICS) triple-bagging technology. Today, PICS bags are being widely adopted in Africa—some 50 million have
been sold so far—and have begun to be adopted in parts of Asia and Central and South America. They are now being promoted around the world
thanks to PICS Global Inc., a spinoff social-benefit company.*

*Starting also in 1987, again encouraged and catalyzed by Lowell, Larry
assembled a team of scientists dedicated to introducing insect-resistance*

genes into cowpea via biotechnology. Cowpea growing in the field is be-
set by insect pests, too, and these were the targets of that work. For many
years Larry led the effort through organizing scientific meetings and rais-
ing funds for research and development. The initiative ultimately proved
successful: In 2018, Nigeria became the first country in the world to release
to its farmers genetically-engineered borer-resistant cowpeas.

How we met

Thanks to winning a USDA grant and publishing papers in Science and in
PNAS after arriving at Purdue in late 1977, I had by 1980 been awarded tenure
and promotion to Associate Professor. What a relief is promotion and tenure!
It freed me to cast about for a long-term project in which I could do good science while maybe helping make the world a little bit better place.

I had, in the meantime, become intrigued by insects that attack stored grain.
Happily, my tolerant and encouraging department head, Eldon Ortman, gave
me substantially free rein to follow my instincts—one of the many blessings
of being at Purdue. Just then my co-worker Dick Shade's former technician,
Laurie Kitch, had decided to study for his Ph.D. and had become John Axtell's
student. Laurie was preparing to leave for Niger, where he planned to breed
cowpeas for resistance to seed beetles called bruchids. Bruchids reproduce at
a frightening rate, and so within two or three months after harvest they can
render a store of cowpea grain full of holed grains, moldy, smelly and worth-
less except to feed chickens and goats.

One day in the early spring of 1982, having been encouraged by Dick Shade,
Laurie knocked cautiously on my office door in the basement of then Entomology Hall. He somewhat bashfully explained that he wanted some technical help in screening cowpea germplasm for resistance to bruchids. He
needed a quick chemical assay, not a long, cumbersome biological one. That
was because he planned to screen many thousands of seed accessions in his
quest to breed bruchid-resistant ones. Would I help? I agreed, but said that
any serious work would require some costs and so would require some modest funding. Laurie's work was at that time supported by a USAID Program
Support grant administered by Lowell. I set up an appointment to meet Lowell and ask for support.

We first met in Lowell's office in the basement of the Ag Administration building. The door was open. I rapped on it politely. Sitting at his desk, he turned toward me and invited me to come in, pointing to a chair. His manner struck me immediately; he was friendly enough but businesslike. I had the feeling right away that I was sitting across from someone whose time was valuable. He had a full head of gray hair, properly combed, and wore a heavy brownish-gray European cut wool business suit. Like the administrator he was, he also wore a tie. I noticed that it was a plaid pattern and remarked that it was a Stewart clan tartan. Smiling, he seemed pleased to tell me that his middle name was Stewart.

As we talked, I couldn't help noticing that, despite the horn-rimmed glasses he was wearing, the pupil of his left eye was clouded over. Our conversation continued. It seemed there was something special about the way he carried himself, something intangible but captivating. The guy had presence, maybe even almost hidden charm. Truth is, at the time I knew almost nothing about Lowell, and I had not taken the trouble to find out. I was not aware that he had recently retired from 17 years as chief agriculturalist with the Ford Foundation, nor did I know that before that he was Head of the Department of Ag Economics. Even so, I was immediately aware that I was talking to a special and unusual man.

After I explained the purpose of my visit, Lowell spent several minutes quizzing me, learning my background, asking about the work I did, learning I was from Linton, in southern Indiana, making me a fellow Hoosier. I was surprised that he seemed to be as interested in me as a person as he was in the matter that had brought me there.

Eventually, while asserting he wasn't a biological scientist, he asked that I tell him about the work I wanted to do with Laurie Kitch, not sparing technical details. After 40 minutes or so, in which I explained what I wanted to do, why, how much money I needed to help Laurie, what the useful outcome might be, plus other details of the little project—like why I wanted to do it—the interview came rather swiftly to an end. Without saying so, he made it clear that he had heard all he needed to hear and that it was time for me to leave. He sat upright in his chair, turned to face me, looked me in the eye and then recited point by point virtually every topic we had covered in our discussion, in one minute at most! I told Laurie later that after Lowell's recitation of the main points of our talk, I felt that he understood what I wanted to do better than I did. Whoa! I walked back to my office in Whistler Hall in a sort of a reverie.

Within a few days I got a handwritten note from Lowell saying that he was allocating $2,000 to the work I had advocated. And so began a working relationship that lasted more than 30 years. Over the next several years he allocated more and more of the funds at his disposal to me. That allowed me to carry out some foundation-laying work and develop some skills that I otherwise could never have done. It also allowed me to invest in colleagues in other departments who had skills I didn't have.

Some things I remember about Lowell

During those years it was not uncommon for me to bump into Lowell in the halls of Purdue's Ag Administration Building. Or on occasion he would drop by to see me at my office in Whistler. We both enjoyed talking Indiana history. He once mentioned his boyhood memories of cultivating corn behind a team of horses. He was then a Quaker lad from Henry County, Indiana. He was proud of his origins, which, though humble enough, were part of the great American farming tradition.

I asked him if he thought he could still hitch up a team of horses. My question was posed at least 75 years after he left the family farm to become a student at Purdue. He acknowledged, modestly, his head thrown back with a distant look in his eye, as if he was watching himself in the long ago, that he believed he could. He'd know how to put on their collars, and string the leather harnesses and attach the double tree; he'd know the horses' names, and what commands to give, the "gee" and "haw" of horse-working language.

Such was the remarkable loom of memories between Lowell's ears, a man so many of us knew as the longtime Assistant Director in Purdue's International Programs in Agriculture. More than once he reflected that agriculture has made great strides since 1917, the year Lowell's memories started their journey of 97 years. Since his birth in the midst of World War I, the USA came to be the earth's granary, not just for storing and providing needed food, but for ideas, values, innovations and inspiration, too. Lowell did his part, far more than most.

Memories of legendary people nestled there in Lowell's head. People like Norman Borlaug, who won the Nobel Peace Prize for spearheading the Green Revolution and saving much of Asia from hunger and even starvation. Lowell and Norm were good friends and sometimes traveled together. While Norm was the star of the team that produced the Green Revolution, the one out front in the spotlight, we need to credit many assists to Lowell, a man who always preferred to stand in the wings, out of the limelight.

I remember him telling me the story—which he later wrote about in his 1999 *Memoir of an International Farmer*—about traveling with Norm Borlaug in India. Late one afternoon, after an exhausting day of dusty travel and work in the countryside, a farmer came and pleaded that Norm come to visit his farm to see his wheat. He said his wheat was sick. Lowell and Norm, alarmed, felt compelled to go see it. They gathered their energy and dragged their tired bodies out to that farm.

They had been tricked. What they were confronted with there on that farm was a celebration, a thanksgiving, for the wheat variety Norm had developed and brought to them. His work had created such prosperity for them that they wanted to show how grateful they were. They presented Norm with a beautiful handmade quilt made of colorful squares stitched together by the women of the many families whose lives had benefited from Norm's wheat. Lowell wrote that tears ran down his cheek that day.

Memories of other extraordinary people resided in Lowell's head. There was Frosty Hill, his first boss during his 16 years with the Ford Foundation. He always spoke fondly of Frosty. He had memories of other bosses, including world figures like Robert McNamara and McGeorge Bundy, both of whom were John F. Kennedy's friends and advisors—the best and the brightest, they have been famously called. Lowell spoke warmly of them, still slightly in awe (you could hear it in his voice), as caring human beings despite their mistakes in the Vietnam War. That was typical of Lowell. He never disparaged anybody.

While with the Ford Foundation, Lowell helped create seven International Agriculture Research Centers, including IITA in Nigeria, CIAT in Colombia, ILRI in Ethiopia, ICARDA in Syria, CIMMYT in Mexico, ICRISAT in India and IFPRI in Washington, D.C. He was one of the architects and founders of some; in others he was one of the master builders and supporters, raising funds and serving on boards.

But Lowell's fondest agricultural memories were of ordinary farmers throughout the world, whether from India, China, Nigeria, Colombia or Brazil. These were people touched by the Green Revolution or by one of the International Centers Lowell helped create. Those people Lowell loved and respected so deeply and sought to help by whatever means he could find. To the end of his life his interest and commitment never wavered. That's why you could still see him in the Ag Administration building sometimes, despite having reached his mid 90s. That's why, when age greatly slowed him down, many of us at Purdue visited Lowell at his home at Westminster Village as often as we could.

What Lowell did for me

He inspired me with his values. We are lucky, he said, and we should give back by unselfishly helping others less lucky. He opened doors for me, enabling me to visit Africa for the first time. He funded my first research related to international agriculture. He critiqued my writings, kindly but firmly pointing out deficiencies. He cried with me when my brilliant son Ian got into trouble, cursed as he was by intractable mental illness that eventually led him to suicide.

Lowell was a great sounding board for ideas. He introduced me to remarkable people who were making a difference in the world, people like Norm Borlaug, Don Paarlberg and John Niederhauser—but there were many more. He cared for others more than anyone I ever met. He taught me—by his example—that if you want to achieve something, you have to find talented people, people with heart, get them engaged, then stand back and let the spotlight shine on them.

He bragged about me to my face sometimes, saying I had a knack for getting people to work together toward a problem much bigger than their academic specialties—but the truth was that I had learned that trick from Lowell. Besides, crafty fellow, he knew his gentle flattery would make me work even harder. It did. He often got me to help without ever asking me or telling me what I should do. Lowell always stood off to the side, avoiding praise. I think he was even annoyed by it and would change the subject quickly.

Larry Murdock and Lowell Hardin at a birthday party in Lowell's honor
organized by Tom Hertel and held at Tom's West Lafayette home.

His courage. Most of all, by his example he gave me courage to dare new things. It wasn't that he was foolhardy, but I remember him telling me how—when he was serving on the board of the International Potato Center (CIP) in Peru—he had to travel with an armed guard into the countryside because the authorities feared that Lowell's team would become a target of the murderous Shining Path. Later, when I traveled in northwest Burkina Faso near the Mali border with an armed guard, I came to better understand Lowell's willingness to take a risk for a good cause.

But I was most struck by another example of Lowell's zest for life, and his readiness to take on new experiences. My wife, Susie, and I had in the early '00s acquired and restored a 1928 open cockpit Travel Air biplane. By 2004 we had been flying it over the agricultural country around Delphi, Indiana, where we kept it in a hangar. This brought us the joy of rare, almost vanished and forgotten experiences that only an open-cockpit airplane can offer: The delightful scent of new-mown hay that rose 1,000 feet above the field, or watching buzzards sweep past us 50 feet below, turning their heads as they passed to get a glimpse of that strange green bird above them. Lowell

Lowell Hardin, 87, ready for takeoff in Larry and Susie Murdock's 1928 Travel Air
4000 open cockpit biplane. During the 30-minute hop up to Lake Freeman and
back, the smile never left his face. He kept this photo on his desk ever after.

Susie and Larry,

Already I've relayed the colorful story of the murder—generated adventure of Saturday to almost everyone I've seen since then. Many first. most recently Don Paarlberg, whose story about his Father's first plane ride you have preserved for posterity.

Thank you both. You have provided me with a memory I shall treasure — especially because you are such generous and treasured friends.

Lowell

seemed intrigued when I told him about our adventures aloft, so one day I asked him if he would like to go for a spin? To my surprise—after all, the man was 87 years old—he smiled broadly and said he'd love to! The following Saturday, after helping Lowell clamber over the leather combing on the edge of the front cockpit, get his seatbelt fastened, and put on a canvas helmet with goggles, we accelerated down the grass runway, the six-cylinder Continental engine making its beautiful roar.

Minutes later we were aloft above Lake Freeman, circling over Lowell and Mary's house a thousand feet below. Mary came out and waved. I could see Lowell leaning over the forward cockpit combing, a great smile on his face, waving back. Landing again at Delphi airport, we disembarked Lowell, whose face was wreathed in smiles. How many 87-year-olds would dare such an adventure? Few. Lowell remains the most elderly passenger I've ever taken for a ride.

On Monday following the Saturday flight, there appeared in my mailbox in Smith Hall a colorful card with a handwritten note (see above). It contained a message of appreciation penned by Lowell shortly after our little adventure. It was for me heartwarming and a treasure, and it was quintessential Lowell Hardin.

Summing up

Lowell's enormous gift was to inspire others, to encourage them, to open doors, to care, as he did for me, to love the farming life, and most of all to help less fortunate people, even and maybe especially those in faraway places. He did all of this virtually without a hint of egotism. Those of us blessed by luck to know Lowell and be mentored by him owe him an enormous debt. How can we make a payment on it? Maybe by writing down what we learned from him, by remembering the example he set, and by passing on the memories.

Shy away from talking about yourself—but certainly never do so in a self-centered way—and by all means fend off praise directed at you.

Suzanne Nielson

Extremely sharp, articulate, and motivating,
but always very humble and modest.

*Dr. Suzanne Nielsen became a faculty member in the Department of Food
Science at Purdue University in 1983, and served as Head of that department from 2003 to 2013. Based on her contributions to teaching of various Food Science courses and the impact of the Food Analysis textbooks
she has edited, she was named a 150th Anniversary Professor at Purdue
in 2018. Prior to becoming Department Head, she had an active research
program in the area of protein chemistry, including the nutrition and utilization of legumes, focused on cowpea and dry bean work for Central
America and Nigeria. Suzanne was involved in international development projects since 1985, including 15 years in the USAID Bean-Cowpea
Collaborative Research Support Program.*

*For the past five years, she has been involved internationally as a
half-time Faculty Fellow in Purdue's Office of Corporate and Global
Partnerships. In that role, she managed the strategic partnership Purdue has with Catholic Relief Services, led an initiative to capitalize on
Purdue's strengths in the area of postharvest loss reduction and value
chain enhancement, and organized the Scale Up Conference at Purdue
on scaling up agricultural technologies and innovations in the developing world. She recently completed the role of Interim Director of the
Purdue-led Feed the Future Food Innovation Lab on Food Processing and
Post-Harvest Handling.*

S hortly after I started a faculty position in 1983, someone referred me
to Larry Murdock, since Larry worked on insects of stored grain, and
how they digest protein. I was interested in the utilization and nutritional quality of legumes, specifically the hard-to-cook defect that can develop

upon storage, and how humans vs. insects digest legume protein. After discussions with Larry, I became part of the RIISP group he organized, an interdepartmental research group to establish host plant resistance against bruchid beetles in cowpeas and common beans.

Larry introduced me to Lowell Hardin, with whom I discussed my research interests and my desire to become involved with the USAID Bean/Cowpea Collaborative Research Program (CRSP). With encouragement and advice from Lowell, I moved forward with my research and association with others who had mutual and complementary interests. This interaction with Lowell no doubt influenced my choice of work over the past 35-plus years. In 1985, I received an IPIA seed grant to work on the hard-to-cook defect of dry beans and cowpeas, and the RIISP group also received an IPIA seed grant. The work made possible through these grants helped make me be competitive in 1986 for IITA funding to work on chemical and physical analysis of improved cowpea lines, and in 1992 for becoming part of a project within the Bean/Cowpea CRSP.

This was the beginning of 15 years of involvement in the Bean/Cowpea CRSP, with my project focused on improving the digestibility and nutritional quality of common bean. My Bean/Cowpea CRSP research was valuable and fulfilling to me, but this project also provided me with extremely valuable leadership experience. Chairing the Technical Committee of the Bean/Cowpea CRSP was valuable for later leadership roles in my career, with many of those related to international development work.

I always thought very highly of Lowell and greatly appreciated his encouragement, support, and mentoring. What an inspiration he was! He was extremely sharp, articulate, and motivating, but he was always very humble and modest. Lowell was very welcoming and genuinely interested in others. He did not seem at all focused on promoting or advancing his own career, but rather on helping others and finding ways to make things happen to benefit others. I remember the seminar series Lowell created to help others learn the international development work and to share ideas. He was very glad to use his extraordinary connections to open doors for others and create opportunities for them. I feel extremely fortunate to have been starting my career when Lowell was so involved with IPIA. I certainly benefited from interacting with Lowell, and he had a significant influence on my life and career path.

Young people don't dwell on the past. They think mostly about the future and savor the delights it may bring. Anyone who does that doesn't grow old.

David Sammons

I was simply dumbfounded that he would even
feel it necessary to ask such a question.

*Following graduation in 1968 with a Biology/Botany degree from Tufts
University, David J. Sammons dedicated most of his career to international education and research in the agricultural sciences. This career
track was launched after two years' service in the Philippines as a Peace
Corps volunteer working with elementary school science teachers. There
he first discerned an interest in agriculture as both a route out of poverty
and a contributor to nutrition and good health in developing countries.*

*Dr. Sammons completed his master's in Economic Botany and, shortly
thereafter, entered a Ph.D. program in Agronomy at the University of Illinois. Completing his Ph.D. in 1978, Dr. Sammons was appointed to a
faculty position in Agronomy/Plant Breeding at the University of Maryland, focused on small grain cereals (wheat and barley). During his tenure at Maryland, Sammons was selected for a Fulbright Award to teach
crop breeding and to contribute to strengthening the crop science curriculum at Egerton College in Kenya while on sabbatical leave in 1986–1987.*

*In 1993, he was appointed Associate Dean and Director of Interna-
tional Programs in Agriculture (IPIA) at Purdue University, a position
that he held until 2006. Through that period, he provided administrative
leadership in the College of Agriculture for USAID-funded, collaborative
research for the improvement of sorghum, peanuts, and cowpeas in East,
Central, and West Africa. Additionally, under his leadership, IPIA initiated study abroad programs in several regions of the world and, at one
point early on, the students in agriculture studying abroad numbered
more than those from any other unit on campus.*

*While at Purdue, Sammons pioneered efforts to add a global dimen-
sion to the Extension component of the land-grant mission by securing
funds to support international activities for Extension educators. His*

support for university engagement with USAID caught the attention of the agency and led to his appointment to a two-year position (2004–2006) in the USAID/Washington Office of Agriculture as a Senior Advisor for University Relations in Teaching, Research, and Extension.

In 2006, Dr. Sammons was recruited to the University of Florida (UF) to lead its office of international programs in the Institute of Food and Agricultural Sciences (IFAS). In that role he led efforts to strengthen IFAS by building an enduring presence for global programs. He has also served on the boards of two international research centers: the International Center for Agricultural Research in the Dry Areas (ICARDA) and the World Vegetable Center (AVRDC), where he served one year as Board Chair. On his retirement from UF in 2013, Dr. Sammons was presented with the UF President's Medallion for significant contributions to advancement of the university's international presence.

I first interacted with Dr. Hardin in 1993, when I was invited to interview for the position of Associate Dean and Director of International Programs in Agriculture (IPIA) at Purdue University. The interview was scheduled in March 1993, shortly after Lowell and his wife, Mary, had been involved in a serious automobile accident. Lowell, consequently, did not participate in the interview, and I did not meet him during that visit. However, after I was offered the position and accepted the appointment, Lowell was the very first person to contact me with his enthusiastic welcome, gracious congratulations, and an offer to support me through the transition to the position. I was touched by his humility and kindness at multiple levels: he was an experienced, well known internationalist; he clearly wanted me to be successful in this new endeavor; he wanted me to feel welcomed and valued as a colleague; he wanted me to develop the same fondness for Purdue that he had; and, finally, he wanted me to know that as an emeritus professor he recognized that I was in charge and he was part of the IPIA staff. His sincere welcome and unpretentiousness was characteristic of our entire friendship and is among my most lasting memories of Lowell.

When I finally had the opportunity to meet Lowell in person, my first impression was that here was a humble and kindly senior faculty member, a deeply experienced professional with immense international insight, and someone who wanted to be helpful as I started my new position. But, of course, Dr. Hardin's role was to be much more than that initial impression might suggest. Over time, he became my mentor, close advisor, professional colleague, and unfailing friend. Lowell was someone I could always turn to for sound insights and good advice. Moreover, our relationship evolved to the point that he would let me know—often unsolicited—when I needed to fix an error, repair a relationship, support a troubled colleague, or clarify any ambiguity with respect to my expectations of staff. He and I had a relationship marked by deep trust and mutual respect that became increasingly important to me through our years together.

Lowell helped advance my career in multiple ways, most prominently through his advice and insight on administrative processes, duties, and responsibilities drawn from his many years in senior leadership positions. He was vocal about the importance of building trusting relationships with those with whom we work, recognizing that there will always be differing opinions—something of value as alternative actions are considered.

I particularly remember his observation that those in leadership positions need to understand that our actions may not always be appreciated by those who report to us, but that we need to be confident about our decisions and able to communicate effectively the reasoning behind those actions. Lowell was clear that competent leaders are not in a popularity contest but that we do need to listen carefully to our colleagues and consider their input as we move toward decisions. He also reminded me of another valuable lesson: those in leadership positions will not always be party to criticisms about what they do—essentially that it can be "lonely at the top," a reality of the leadership role even though it can be troubling.

All of these qualities and values were embodied by Lowell in his own professional work and contributed to his immense stature in the world of international agriculture. These lessons, observations, and values informed my development as a successful campus leader both at Purdue and later at the University of Florida.

Additionally, Lowell helped advance my career through pushing me in new directions. Sensing that my experience and interests would be potentially beneficial to the global agricultural research community, Lowell proposed (without my knowing it) my candidacy for a seat on the board of one of the international agricultural research centers within the CG system. His prominence and enormous experience with the CG and broadly in global agricultural research gave my nomination credibility that otherwise it would never have had. That nomination led directly to my election to the Board of Trustees of the International Center for Agricultural Research in the Dry Areas (ICARDA), a seat I held for six years, beginning in 2004. Subsequently, I was elected to the Board of Directors of The World Vegetable Center (AVRDC) and served there for eight years (one year as Board Chair) beginning in 2010. Of note, one of the thrilling discoveries early in my tenure on the ICARDA Board was seeing Lowell Hardin's name on a plaque in the headquarters building, recognizing him as one of the founders of that center many years before my formal role there!

Beyond my professional engagement with Lowell, my family also connected with him in varying positive and important ways. Part of my role as Associate Dean and Director of IPIA was hosting prominent international visitors, often at dinners in our home. This imposed significant responsibility on my wife, Becky, who assumed these duties always with grace but at times with some trepidation as well. Lowell was generally a guest at these events and would unfailingly praise Becky for the menu prepared, the items served, and the warm hospitality. One particularly challenging guest from India who, together with his wife, had demanding food preferences, was presented with a meal that Becky had researched with much care, and Lowell, typically as always, was especially complimentary of her meeting that test with great success!

Our younger daughter, who worked as a food service employee at Westminster Village in West Lafayette, a senior life care community where Lowell and Mary lived, also developed a friendship with Lowell. (She always addressed him as "Dr. Hardin," noting the great respect with which he was held by all of the Westminster staff). Lowell, of course, always had nice things to say to and about her, something that she and my wife and I treasured.

Finally, an anecdote to finish this essay: Lowell, in his capacity as professor emeritus, worked in the IPIA office for many unpaid hours during my tenure, and I enjoyed seeing him on a regular basis. One dreary winter day in West Lafayette, Lowell came into my office and asked if I had a few minutes to talk.

He told me of plans that he and Mary had made to travel to Arizona to spend several weeks in the warmth and sunshine there, far from another Hoosier winter. His question: Would that absence be acceptable to me as office director? Could he have some time off?

I was simply dumbfounded that he would even feel it necessary to ask such a question, responding that of course it was absolutely fine. I told him that every time he walked through the IPIA office door was a blessing to me. And that is as true now as it was then. He was a unique and remarkable human being, and the time we shared will always be important to me, as I know it has been to many around the world.

Of course, say "Thank you" when someone helps you or does you a favor. A phone call is better than an email. A handwritten note expressing your appreciation is still better. Best of all, go and knock on their door and thank them eye to eye.

Gerald "Jerry" Shively

Lowell's method was never to tear
somebody down. Just the opposite.

Jerry Shively is an award-winning applied economist with more than two decades of international experience. He currently serves as Associate Dean in the College of Agriculture at Purdue University, where he is also Director of International Programs in Agriculture (IPIA). His career has been devoted to teaching and conducting policy-oriented research focused on improving global food and nutrition security and promoting the sustainability of smallholder agriculture. He has published more than 100 scholarly works and for nine years served as Editor-in-Chief of the journal Agricultural Economics, the flagship journal of the International Association of Agricultural Economists.

He is the recipient of numerous teaching and research awards, including the 2007 Purdue College of Agriculture Outstanding Researcher award. In 2008 he was named a Purdue University Faculty Scholar, and in 2018 received the Distinguished Graduate Teaching Award from the Agricultural and Applied Economics Association. He is a faculty affiliate of the Purdue Policy Research Institute, a Purdue Faculty Fellow for Global Affairs, and serves on the Executive Committee of Purdue's Center for Global Food Security. In 2016 he was named a Fellow of the African Association of Agricultural Economists, and in 2018 was made an Honorary Life Member of the International Association of Agricultural Economists. He received his Ph.D. in Agricultural and Applied Economics from the University of Wisconsin–Madison in 1996.

I met Lowell soon after arriving at Purdue as a young Assistant Professor in 1996. At the time, I didn't know much about Lowell's background and didn't fully appreciate the depth of his experience or his influence in international circles. By then, he was a Professor Emeritus and—from my naïve and uninformed perspective—simply one of the many graybeards floating around the College of Agriculture.

In those days, Lowell presided over an informal monthly gathering of colleagues working on international agricultural topics. Most of the time, the meeting followed a seminar-like format. Unlike department seminars, however, it was attended by colleagues from numerous departments. Today, I suppose we'd call it interdisciplinary, but I don't think that label was being used very much at the time. This was in the days before Purdue's Discovery Park had been established, with its multiple centers pulling faculty in several directions at once, and Lowell's gatherings attracted a wide range of researchers. It was an intellectual watering hole, where a broad collection of the college's species came to drink of knowledge, among them animal scientists, economists, entomologists, foresters and plant breeders.

Participating in these get-togethers gave me some of my first real and serious exposure to work outside of economics. It was also formative, both in terms of providing the broad context that would inform my professional career and my participation in agricultural research projects, and in terms of setting a tone for collegiality and mutual respect for what others could bring to the conversation.

I quickly came to realize that Lowell was a special person—a kind of human superglue that held everyone together. His infectious spirit, his can-do optimism, and his unbridled enthusiasm for everyone and everything was a large part of his appeal. Somehow, he never let his deep knowledge and broad experience take the spotlight. Instead, he was at his happiest when shining the light on others. In those days, I didn't bring much to the table. I had worked in only a few countries—primarily the Philippines, for my dissertation—and had really only worked on a few narrow topics. My field of vision was pretty narrow, and I can only guess that I probably said a lot of things that, to Lowell, with his many years of experience and broad perspective, didn't make sense.

But Lowell's method was never to tear somebody down. Just the opposite. I remember giving a seminar once about some work that I had done on irrigation in a rice-growing area of southern Palawan, a remote and rarely visited corner of the Philippines. Afterward, Lowell came up to me and said, without a hint of sarcasm or insincerity, "That was absolutely the best seminar on the topic I've ever heard. Fantastic work! An absolutely terrific presentation!" He was effusive in his praise and made me feel like a million bucks.

Looking back, I can see that he could undoubtedly speak with conviction because my seminar was the only one he had ever heard on irrigated rice production in southern Palawan. But that was his way: he was always trying to build people up and bring out their best, inspiring them to do more and work harder—not by cajoling, but by appealing to a person's inner desire to do better and contribute more.

In truth, I interacted with Lowell relatively little down through the years. Nevertheless, he possessed a charisma that could leave a strong mark from even casual encounters. Down through the years, I've drawn a lot of inspiration from Lowell's example. At times, I've heard his voice; and in my memory, I've seen his sprite-like smile encouraging me to do more, and to do it better. Now that I'm Director of IPIA, walking the halls that he once walked, I find myself reminded of him on an almost daily basis, thinking about how I might follow his example in some small way, with the hope of bringing to others his passion, enthusiasm and concern for the world and all the people in it.

Care about the people you are mentoring. Treat them with the same amount of caring you would for your son or daughter.

Wally Tyner

Always there when needed but never tried to impose his views.

Tyner joined the Purdue faculty in 1977 after earning his bachelor's degree in chemistry from Texas Christian University and his master's and doctoral degrees from the University of Maryland. For 13 years, from 1989 to 2002, Tyner served as Head of the Department of Agricultural Economics at Purdue, and the department grew in stature nationally and internationally.

During his 42-year tenure at Purdue, Tyner earned a global reputation for his extensive research in the areas of energy, agriculture, climate and natural resource policy analysis and his incisive ability to apply that research to current issues and challenges. He earned the trust of leaders in the U.S. Congress, the White House and many foreign countries. He was routinely interviewed by major media outlets from around the world. Tyner's many honors include being named an energy patriot by late U.S. Sen. Richard Lugar, an honorary life member of the International Association of Agricultural Economics, a 2019 senior fellow for the United States Association for Energy Economics, and a fellow of the American Association for the Advancement of Science and the Agricultural and Applied Economics Association.

I have had so many encounters with Lowell Hardin over the years, I cannot remember the first, but I can remember some that made the strongest impression on me. Very shortly after I became department head, Lowell came into my office for a chat, and I asked him for advice. He humbly replied that things had changed since he was department head, so any advice he might have would be outdated.

Then he went on to add two key pieces of advice that I tried to follow throughout my years as department head. First, Lowell told me that he had always believed that a department chair should comport like a department head, and a department head like a department chair. Of course, what Lowell was saying is yes, you have a lot of power as department head—much more than as a chair, but exercise of that power is best managed as if you were a department chair. Lowell was spot-on. The second piece of advice he provided was that as a department head you need to lead, you need to be out front of the faculty—but not too far in front. You need to bring the faculty along with you.

Those two nuggets of wisdom helped guide my daily actions for years. But Lowell's help and guidance did not stop there. Lowell would occasionally drop by my office just to chat. He usually began by apologizing for interrupting my work, and I always replied that I would gain more from interacting with him than in whatever else I could do in that time. Our chats ranged over a wide variety of topics. Sometimes there was no clear agenda. At other times, he would work around to getting my opinion on some topic, which often was a subtle way to provide me some sound advice on that topic.

Sometimes after faculty meetings or other events, I would get a note from Lowell written in a style and communicating as no one else could. In particular, I remember the note he sent after the faculty meeting in which the Dean came over to announce that I was stepping down as department head. Lowell described the rush of emotion as the entire faculty joined in a standing ovation for my time as their leader. He said it much better than I ever could, and it was just an example of the continuous encouragement and support Lowell provided. After I finished my sentence as department head, Lowell continued to drop by for chats. He seemed genuinely interested in the research, teaching, and Extension activities in which I was involved. I have been very fortunate in my career to have support from my family, my colleagues, our support staff, and many others. Lowell Hardin was always there when needed but never tried to impose his views. He was a mentor in the very finest sense of that word, and there is no way to understate the value of that mentorship and friendship.

Editors' note: After contributing this essay, Wally Tyner passed away unexpectedly on August 25, 2019. This was a great loss to the Purdue family.

Being on time and starting promptly at the agreed-upon hour is not to be a slave to the clock. It is, rather, an act of respect and even honor, for the speaker, for the listeners or for the person you are meeting.

PART 3

Friends

Bill Butz

Lowell Hardin cleaned his plate.

William Butz is an economic demographer, survey director, statistical system administrator, science policy and nonprofit administrator, and policy advisor. He was, from April 2011 to October 2013, a Senior Research Scientist with the World Population Program at the International Institute for Applied Systems Analysis (IIASA) in Austria, where he helped direct research applying tools of demography to challenges of human capital formation around the world. Previously, he was President/CEO of the Population Reference Bureau in Washington (2003–2011), Senior Economist at the RAND Corporation (2002–2003, 1970–1983), Senior Resident Consultant at the Futures Group (2002), Division Director for Social and Economic Sciences at the National Science Foundation (1995–2001), and Associate Director for Demographic Programs at the U.S. Census Bureau (1983–1995). His undergraduate and graduate studies at Indiana University and the University of Chicago were in economics.

His own research, published in more than 50 peer-reviewed articles, monographs and book chapters, has focused on economic and demographic aspects of poverty, fertility, mortality, nutrition, education, and scientific manpower in developing countries, the U.S. and Europe. He directed survey projects in Guatemala and Malaysia, taught economic development at UCLA, was a member of the Board of Reviewing Editors of Science magazine from 2002 to 2013, and is a fellow of the American Statistical Association and the American Association for the Advancement of Science.

L owell Hardin cleaned his plate. Not a sliver of fat left from that T-bone steak grilled in their backyard across the lane from our house. My 10-year-old eyes looked over from my hacked-up platter with wonder and a little apprehension. Probably, I hid my mess with a napkin.

It is not a stretch to call that mentoring. Lowell (we kids called each other's parents by their first names, a rare privilege) didn't admonish me to clean my plate. Not then nor in any future meals when his waste-not example was too strict for me to follow. He didn't have to. What is responsible, correct, was clear.

In high school, the two sons challenged their dads on the links. Lowell's play was distinguished in three respects: his ball generally headed toward the hole, his swing raced without a hitch around his head to where it began, and he took the game seriously. I'm not sure it was a game with Lowell. He didn't seem to be competing with anyone, instead studying every shot to improve the next one. I distinctly remember the absence of small talk on an afternoon I thought was made for fun.

In fact, in my growing-up years I don't remember small talk at all from Lowell Hardin. It was prices and policy in Washington and the world, staffing and teaching in the department and the university, and process and outcome on the football field and basketball court. More of the first than the second and more of the second than the third.

(The story goes that son Tom asked his high school teacher a question about economics. The teacher suggested that Tom's father was a professor of agricultural economics at Purdue, why not ask him? "I don't want to know that much about it," Tom replied. The ring of truth.)

All that dinner table talk of agricultural prices and policy bored this teenager until the first university economics class. My direction was clear from then on. Lowell took delight. What courses was I taking? What parts did I like? Were there examples from agriculture? How were the profs? Among my father's many professional friends, Lowell was one of only two who engaged me seriously, even more than my father did. Professor Hardin actually wanted to discuss this stuff with me! I don't remember being flattered as much as encouraged, propelled on to learn these tools, expecting their usefulness.

By the senior year there was only one university I wanted to attend for graduate study and one professor I wanted mainly to study with. In a conversation I still remember, Lowell confirmed my interest while defining the odd angle into agricultural economics that would be featured with Ted Schultz at the University of Chicago. Several years later I happened to see the letter Lowell wrote Professor Schultz on my behalf. I had had no idea. Nor do I have any idea what other letters Lowell may have written for me over the years.

Lowell's interest in what I was doing and thinking only increased during my Chicago years. What was I reading, what was I writing, was I going to take a course with professor so-and-so? By this time, I was questioning Lowell in return. Only years later did he reveal his concern—to put it mildly—with the technical turn of agricultural economics journals. In those years, though, not a word of disparagement of the econometrics and mathematical modeling I was telling him about.

While Lowell was around the world with the Ford Foundation and I was directing projects in Guatemala and Malaysia, our infrequent times together were the same as always: serious, reflective, interactive. Now and then he got hold of a publication of mine and sent me a note. In the middle of this period, the U.S. Census Bureau offered me a job in Washington: leading 850 staff rather than a handful at RAND, directing budgets of hundreds of millions rather than thousands, scurrying to meetings rather than specifying computer runs, contending with Washington bureaucracy rather than Santa Monica beaches, maybe even speaking to congressional committees rather than professional gatherings. In every respect an enormous change for career and family.

Lowell and Mary Hardin had faced the same kind of challenge, I remembered, when they left Purdue and West Lafayette for Ford Foundation and the world: the same uncertainties and downright unknowns. We had never talked about their decision, but now we did. My excitement must have been palpable and Lowell clearly shared it, in spite of trying to appear analytical.

My family made the move and, except for finishing some pipeline articles, I never looked back. When I think about all the talks with Lowell, it is this one, this hinge in my life, that is most vivid. Out of his personal history and our relationship, he gave me confidence to do what I wanted to do. He knew I could make the leap. From that point on, I have always felt Lowell's pride in me. Even when I have faltered badly, I knew he believed in me. That has always mattered.

In later years, I never entered his home without serious submersion into one intersection after another of his interests and my work. First, we would review how our families were doing. Lowell loved all of mine. Amid the joys, even this was serious. Boy, I loved these conversations! Leaning forward in his chair, so did Lowell. He asked me to speak before his International Seminar at Purdue. That Lowell led this high-powered group of colleagues deep into his retirement years is a mentoring example that still admonishes me.

On one such visit, I noticed *Science* magazines in his chair-side stack. We agreed that neither of us understood much of the contents anymore, but still enjoyed it. Having recently been elected a Fellow of the American Association for the Advancement of Science, which publishes the journal, it occurred to me that Lowell Hardin should be an AAAS Fellow also, primarily for his Green Revolution contributions. I assembled the necessary materials that passed him easily through the election.

Lowell was pleased. I thought back to that letter he wrote to the University of Chicago . . . but didn't mention it. Now I think back to his clean dinner plates of my childhood. Other plates—of intellectual energy, social contribution, mentoring of others—have never been "clean," always brimming full. Where his influence will end cannot be ciphered.

Encourage new ideas, explore them with the person you are mentoring. Be positive. Be ready and willing to get excited.

Leon Hesser

Our wives heard us giggling.

Leon F. Hesser is an American international agricultural development specialist. He grew up on a farm in Indiana. He served in the U.S. Army as a teenage soldier in the Philippines during World War II. He was awarded both the Combat Infantry Badge and the Combat Medic Badge. When the war ended, he served with the Army of Occupation in Japan. The differences in the cultures and the agriculture in the Philippines and Japan from those which he had grown up with in the Midwest of the United States fascinated him and stimulated him to embark on a career of international agricultural development.

Hesser received B.S. (1958), M.S. (1960), and Ph.D. (1962) degrees in agricultural economics from Purdue University. He joined the Foreign Service of the United States in 1966 as director of America's program to help increase food production in the then hungry nation of Pakistan. In 1973, he transferred to the U.S. Department of State in Washington, D.C., as director of America's worldwide program of agricultural technical assistance for developing countries. He took early retirement in 1978 and until the year 2000 served as a consultant in various countries of Asia, Africa, and the former Soviet Union.

As Director of the Office of Agriculture in the Agency for International Development in Washington from 1973 to 1978, Hesser managed five divisions—crops, livestock, soil & water, economics, and fisheries—of specialists who served on call to analyze and provide assistance to problems in agricultural development in countries of Asia, Africa, and Latin America.

*Much of the technical assistance was marshaled through 75 to 80 contracts
that the Office had with American universities and research institutions.
The Office of Agriculture also had responsibility for managing the U.S. financial input into the then-growing set of international agricultural research centers under the umbrella of the Consultative Group for International Agricultural Research (CGIAR).*

*Between 1978 and 2000, Hesser served as an agricultural development
consultant in Bangladesh, Afghanistan, Kenya, Malawi, Zambia, Swazi-
land, Egypt, St. Vincent and the Grenadines, Russia, Ukraine, Hungary,
Albania, and Poland.*

L owell was head of the Agricultural Economics Department when I was a 30-year-old freshman in Agricultural Economics at Purdue in 1955. Shortly after I received the B.S. degree in 1958, in an evening ceremony of students and staff of Ag Economics, Lowell presented to me a certificate indicating that I had received the highest grade average for Ag Econ grads in 1958. I was dumbfounded, because I had had no idea beforehand. But he encouraged me to continue.

I was halfway through the master's degree when Lowell had been asked by Earl Butz, who was then U.S. Secretary of Agriculture, to go during the summer of 1960 to Japan for three months to do an assessment of America's Public Law 480—Food for Peace—program in Japan. Lowell, who knew of my interest in foreign agriculture and who knew that I had been in Japan for six months with the Army of Occupation, asked if I would be interested in accompanying him on the assignment. Of course, I jumped at the chance. Our wives went along. It was a terrific experience, not only for the technical aspects of the assignment, but also for the personal experience for my wife and me in close association with Lowell and Mary Hardin.

Upon arriving in Japan, we checked in with Dr. Chuck Elkinton, Chief of USAID's Agriculture Division, and outlined a plan of work for the summer. My working as Lowell's assistant during the next three months was indeed stimulating. But let me mention just one interesting event. As one of our duties, Lowell and I were invited one night to a geisha party. We had only small amounts of saki, but it was enough that our wives, who were on the second floor of International House, heard us giggling as we came in the front door. When we got up to the room, Mary said to Lowell, "Tell us about the party—was it suggestive?" Lowell said, "Oh, no. One of the girls said, 'Tell me about ag-re-cul-tur-al ec-o-nom-ics.' Mary, who had never been known to swear, shouted, "Oh, hell." That summer was the beginning of a very close, lifelong friendship between the Hessers and the Hardins.

Helping others, particularly the young but anyone who needs a helping hand or a shoulder to lean on, closes the door to growing old.

Rob Paarlberg

A most unusual gift—a paperback copy
of *Lady Chatterley's Lover*.

Robert Paarlberg is Adjunct Professor of Public Policy at the Harvard Kennedy School of Government and a Research Associate at Harvard's Weatherhead Center for International Affairs. He is also Emeritus Professor of Political Science at Wellesley College. He received his B.A. from Carleton College and a Ph.D. in International Relations from Harvard University, and is the author of six university press books, including Starved for Science: Keeping Biotechnology out of Africa (Harvard 2008) and Food Politics: What Everyone Needs to Know (Oxford 2013). Paarlberg has been a member of the Board of Agriculture and Natural Resources at the National Research Council of the National Academies, and was a member of the Board of Directors of Winrock International. He has been a consultant to the International Food Policy Research Institute, USAID, the Chicago Council on Global Affairs, the Aspen Institute, and the Bill and Melinda Gates Foundation. On half a dozen occasions he has testified to Congress, and he now chairs the Independent Steering Committee for the CGIAR research program on Agriculture for Nutrition and Health. Paarlberg's new book, to be published in 2020 by Knopf, will be titled Resetting the Table: Straight Talk About the Food We Grow and Eat.

My close relationship with Lowell Hardin did not develop until years after our first encounter, since I was just an infant when we first met. Lowell and Mary Hardin were the closest of friends with my own mom and dad, first at Purdue in the late 1930s when Dad and Lowell were fraternity brothers, and then once more at Cornell as graduate students.

My first lasting memory of Lowell dates from when I was in my early teens, living in Washington, D.C., where Dad was working for the Eisenhower Administration. Lowell had arrived from out of town for a visit, and brought for me and my older brother a most unusual gift—a paperback copy of D. H. Lawrence's erotic novel, *Lady Chatterley's Lover*, until that time unavailable in the United States, since it had been banned for obscenity. Thinking back, this was an odd choice since Lowell must have known my parents were somewhat prudish. Perhaps this was his effort at supplementary parenting. In any case, it served as a worthy contribution to my early education.

My family moved back to West Lafayette when I was in high school, and long before I developed an adult relationship with Lowell I became a close school friend with his older son, Tom. The summer after I graduated from college, Tom and I even hitchhiked around Australia together. Lowell had moved to New York by then to work at Ford, but he went out of his way to stay in touch, inviting me on one occasion to an elegant dinner at his spacious sixth-floor apartment on East 77th Street. In this fancy neighborhood, Lowell somehow fit right in. He was always an immaculate dresser, perfectly groomed and barbered. I almost never saw Lowell without a tie. In a tailored suit, wearing eyeglasses, and with a high part that showed off his full head of hair, Lowell looked more like an attorney or a banker than a boy from the farm. The one mystery to his appearance was a stubby middle finger on his left hand. He cheerfully explained that he got it when the horse-drawn cultivator he was riding with his dad suddenly hit a rock; missing fingers were an all-too-common badge of honor for farm boys at the time.

My early graduate work was focused on American foreign policy, not agriculture, but that didn't stop Lowell from taking an interest. Even after I drifted away from my friendship with his son Tom, Lowell kept me in his orbit. By the time I took my first job teaching international relations at Wellesley College, my research interests began gravitating back to international food and agriculture, influenced by my dad's distinguished academic and governmental career in that area. My dad, Don Paarlberg, had achieved considerable prominence as an award-winning teacher at Purdue, a writer of multiple books on farm policy, and most of all as a senior government official, including sub-Cabinet positions at USDA and a stint as an assistant to the president in the White House. With all this, Dad never did develop Lowell's deep interest in building personal networks, supporting the growth of institutions, and in mentoring people, all of the areas where Lowell excelled. When Lowell noticed my interests were turning toward international agriculture, he spotted another chance to do some supplementary parenting, helping where he could to move my career along.

I never knew for sure all that Lowell did for me, because he never shared any details, probably to protect me from the self-doubt that might creep in if I knew I was getting an unearned advantage. Still, some good fortune I had early was likely due to Lowell's hidden hand. When I applied to the Ford Foundation for a small grant to travel to India to do research for my first book, the grant came through. When I applied to be a scholar-in-residence at the Rockefeller Foundation's conference and study center in Bellagio, I was successful. When I was asked out of the blue to do some work for BIFAD, and then to chair a review of the CRSPs, and then to serve on the Board at Winrock International in Arkansas, it wasn't hard to guess who had put my name into the hat. When I was then invited to perform a series of tasks at IFPRI, Lowell must have once again been on the phone to someone.

I did not appreciate the full weight of Lowell's opinion inside the CGIAR system until, on one occasion, I found myself at IFPRI headquarters in Washington trying to finish a report I had been asked to draft on the Institute's research methodologies. I needed somewhere quiet to sit, so a staff assistant was told by the Director to take me down the hall to a large and completely empty corner office, one that offered generous views of gleaming buildings and flowering trees on the city streets far below. As the assistant opened the door to bring me in, she explained with a hushed reverence, "This is Doctor Hardin's office."

For all this, the only thing Lowell wanted back from me was to report periodically on what I was doing and on what his many other friends and protégés in the world of international agriculture were up to. Well into his final years, Lowell took pride as well as pleasure in having up-to-date information, straight from the front lines. Sometimes I would brief him one-to-one from the easy chair in his living room at Westminster Village, but just as often it would be over lunch at the Purdue Memorial Union, where Lowell would often bring along someone else he wanted me to meet. This is how I was able to form valuable relationships with Will Masters, Gebisa Ejeta, Larry Murdock, and Tom Hertel, all Lowell's friends and an A-list of today's experts in international agriculture. Lowell also invited me to present at his brown-bag lunch seminar whenever I came to West Lafayette, even when I had nothing new to say. He never let me pay for anything, explaining that the "Hardin Foundation" would cover the expense.

Lowell Hardin was most relaxed—finally without a tie—at his house on Lake Freeman, particularly when presiding over summertime dinners for friends and family on his rustic screen porch. Simply being close to the lake remained a tonic for him. On one unique occasion later in his life, a lunch was arranged by Bill Butz, Earl's oldest son, near the lake at the Sportsman Inn, in a sunny room overlooking the Tippecanoe River. Earl Butz, my dad, and Lowell Hardin were all growing old together at Westminster Village, and Bill thought they would enjoy a group excursion. With these three aging heavyweights sitting around a big table, joined by a small but appreciative audience that included Bill and me, the conversation ranged widely over the entire eight or nine decades of agricultural history these men had witnessed together—and decisively shaped. The waitress eventually cleared all the dishes, and the other diners in the room were all gone by midafternoon, but these three men still had things to say, so the seminar continued. Earl was being slightly competitive, as usual, and Dad was willing to interrupt when he didn't like something Earl had said, which was also in character. Lowell also played to form, serving as the peacemaker, reacting to everything with expressive smiles, or frowns, and taking care all the while to keep the conversation moving forward.

From his unique position in the foundation world, Lowell Hardin was the kingpin of a highly influential (and mostly like-minded) postwar Ag Mafia, made powerful by its scientific and academic grounding at land-grant universities like Purdue and Cornell, and uniquely credible due to the on-farm experience of its most senior members. This was a network that brought a forward-looking vision to government agencies like USDA and USAID, and one that gave to the world a network of international agricultural research centers. These were institutions that Lowell, most of all, had helped to build. Lowell knew the importance of his role in this network, but he did not hoard the influence it conferred. Instead, he was eager to bring in anyone who showed a good-faith interest in the larger common mission: helping farmers in poor as well as rich countries escape hunger and poverty.

Become part of the lives of those you are mentoring. And don't forget that they are not islands unto themselves but have families, with whom they share concerns, joys, feelings and troubles. Care for your mentees. And for their families.

Marge Stacey

Lowell didn't get to see what I have done.

Marge was Lowell's faithful caretaker for the last several years of his life. A farm girl raised in rural Indiana who never finished high school, she cooked a main meal for him daily, accompanied him shopping for groceries, and took him to visit the doctor. Each member of this partnership deeply appreciated what the other did for them.

L owell Hardin and I met when he was in his 90s. I was in my 40s. I got acquainted with an amazing man. He became a big influence in helping me get education and a career in mid-life.

I was a caregiver for Lowell for almost his entire last four years. He was such a caring person. He made all his guests know who I was, too. We cried together, laughed together, and enjoyed the view from the dining room table of his cottage at Westminster Village in West Lafayette. We talked together about many things, like growing up on a farm. He was from Henry County and I was from Benton County.

He became like a father to me.

In all our talk it was striking that all of his children and grandchildren had gone to college. I didn't go past junior year in high school. I raised a family. And I never made enough money working. When I worked with Lowell, I was getting paid only $10 an hour by the home care agency that employed me.

Lowell didn't say directly I should get further education. But he said I had so much to offer. He said I should write a book about all my years doing home care. And he encouraged me a lot. He basically said that if you don't reach for higher goals, you can't get them. He asked if I thought I could do going back to school, after I was out of school for 33 years. I came to believe that if you don't have education, you're not going to get farther than where you are.

I decided to get my GED. When I got my grades, Lowell was so proud of me.

After Lowell had a stroke, I was thinking of getting even further education. I decided to do it. I made my final decision after he died in March 2015, and the home care agency told me I wasn't worth more than $10 an hour.

I left the agency. I applied to Ivy Tech to study in human services. I started there in September 2015, going to school by day and working by night. I lived with my daughter for two and a half years to save money.

I graduated from Ivy Tech at age 54 in 2017. In my last semester I had an internship at the Wabash Center, and I liked it a lot. Then I worked at Wabash Center as a Direct Support Person, helping people who have special needs and mental illness. Now I am lead DSP, the house manager of 13 people who live in the community on their own. Eventually I'd like to become program manager.

My work at Wabash Center does my heart joy. One recent day I helped a consumer go shopping for a microwave and some new clothes. When he took it out of the box at his home, his smile was so big you would have thought I just handed him a million dollars.

Lowell didn't get to see what I have done. But in a way, he has been walking with me all through this. I talk to people about him all the time. He was one in a million.

You don't have to be the smartest person in the room to make a valuable contribution to the discussion. Harvesting sincere and diverse perspectives will result in the best possible outcome.

Tim Wallace

He's actually listening to you. You are also aware that his expectations are high.

Tim Wallace considers himself a "Yes man"—not a person who caves into other people's demands, but the kind who says "Yes" to life. He is Professor Emeritus from UC Berkeley, where he served as an Extension Specialist focusing on natural resource management.

Tim has also served as president of the Claremont Canyon Conservancy, which works to make the neighborhood more fire-safe and a more enjoyable place to live. The organization's goals are wildfire risk reduction, trail development, natural landscape restoration, and educational tours of the canyon led by experts. "Working with volunteers, we have helped make the canyon more fire-safe, more natural, and more accessible by trails."

Tim has been involved with natural resources all his life: first as rancher and logger, then later in academics. He has been at UC Berkeley since 1963. "I've worked at the White House on agricultural matters and was Director of California's Department of Food and Agriculture. I've done consulting abroad in Europe, Latin America, Africa, the Far East, and New Zealand and Australia." He has a Ph.D. from Purdue in agricultural economics. A specialty of his is facilitating group conflicts about land/water use. "I like to get out and work on real-world problems." One of his proudest achievements was going into ranching and logging straight from graduating from Harvard at age 20. "I was the only person in my class that, upon graduation, went into any sort of agriculture."

Lowell's and my lives have touched off and on for over 65 years. Upon meeting him you're immediately aware he's actually listening to you. You are also aware that his expectations are high, and so you try to elevate your conversation to intentionally say something meaningful.

Lowell was recruiting at an AAEA annual meeting in the mid-1950s for his Purdue Department, and I was job hunting. My wife, two young ones and a third on the way were all in on our possible move from Nevada to Indiana to get a job, degree and future. He and I visited about the prospective job in Rural Development, a possible way to work on a degree, what I could do to bring credits I'd earned, and salary. We'd about come to the end of the conversation when I said, "I need more—as much as I can get." Lowell didn't blink, and then came up with a larger number. We shook hands.

With me working full-time, he encouraged me to do the degree quickly to start the academic climb. He taught me to write, not the academic way but for readership understanding and brevity. In the best sense of the word, Lowell was an "enabler."

He was remarkable in being able to spot talent, give it full rein, and then see to it that that talent got recognized widely by others who could, in turn, open other doors. All of us who were asked to write something for this work are beneficiaries of his largesse.

He was a generous man with his time, ideas and contacts. Along my way he also shared his house and family. I'll never forget an invitation to his place on an Indiana lake during a critically humid and hot summer there.

He liked decision-makers who could look at a situation, see what was needed and resolve it quickly. Upon arrival in West Lafayette, we needed better transportation, having exhausted our current secondhand car by hauling a very heavily loaded trailer 2,000 miles, plus we needed a place to live. Both were obtained within a couple of days, and Lowell was impressed.

He was also a family man and was often caught between a professional commitment and family desires. We all know that miserable place. And Mary was true to him always as wife and nurse during his physical issues at Purdue, in New York or while traveling worldwide.

I'm still benefiting from my years of association with Lowell—and as always, I couldn't find a way to pay him back except continue to try my best, remain ethical, and extend a helping hand whenever I could, hoping it would reflect back positively on my dear friend and mentor.

Lowell was a true gentleman—a very gentle, persuasive, far-seeing person who helped me tremendously and is still doing so. God bless him and all those he helped, as they are still spreading his good influences.

Appendices

Acronyms

ADB: Asian Development Bank
AAAS: American Association for the Advancement of Science
AAEA: Agricultural & Applied Economics Association
CGIAR: Consultative Group for International Agricultural Research
CIAT: Centro Internacional de Agricultura Tropical
CIMMYT: Centro Internacional de Mejoriamento de Maiz y Trigo
CIP: Centro Internacional de la Papa
CIRAD: Centre de Cooperation Internationale en Recherche Agronomique
   pour le Developpement
CRSP: Collaborative Research Support Program
FAO: Food and Agriculture Organization
GTA: Global Trade Analysis Project
ICARDA: International Center for Agricultural Research in the Dry Areas
ICRISAT: International Crops Research Institute for the Semi-Arid Tropics
IFPRI: International Food Policy Research Institute
IITA: International Institute of Tropical Agriculture
ILCA: International Livestock Centre for Africa
ILRI: International Livestock Research Institute
IPIA: International Programs in Agriculture (Purdue)
IRD: Institut de la Recherche pour le Developpement
IRRI: International Rice Research Institute
IWMI: International Water Management Institute
OCP: Office Cherifien des Phosphates
OECD: Organisation for Economic Co-operation and Development
PNAS: Proceedings of National Academy of Science
RAND: Research and Development Corporation
RIISP: Research Initiative: Insects of Seeds and Plants
TAC: Technical Advisory Committee
USAID: United States Agency for International Development

USDA: United States Department of Agriculture
UNDP: United Nations Development Program
WFP: World Food Program

Lowell S. Hardin

Curriculum Vitae in Brief

Emeritus Professor of Agricultural Economics
Purdue University
International Programs in Agriculture
West Lafayette, IN 47907–2053

Born
November 16, 1917; Henry County, Indiana
Son of J. Fred and Mildred (Stewart) Hardin

Education
B.S.A., Purdue University, 1939
Ph.D., Cornell University, 1943

Married
Mary Cooley of West Lafayette, Indiana; September 21, 1940

Experience
Reared on general livestock farm
Field inspector, Indiana Crop Improvement Associate, summer 1938
Managing Editor, *Purdue Exponent*, daily student publication, 1939
Graduate assistant, Cornell University, 1939–43
Assistant Director, National Agricultural Work Simplification Project and Instructor, Purdue University, 1943–44
Assistant, Associate Professor, Purdue University, 1944–49
Professor, Purdue University, 1950–53
Head of Department of Agricultural Economics, Purdue University, 1953–65
Senior Agriculturalist, Office of Vice President, International Division, Ford Foundation, 1965–81

Assistant Director, International Programs in Agriculture, Purdue University, 1981–2007

Emeritus Professor, Purdue University, 2007–2015

Professional memberships

American Agricultural Economics Association

International Association of Agricultural Economics

American Association for the Advancement of Science

Areas of teaching and research specialization

Farm Management

Production Economics

Agricultural Policy

Agricultural Development

Publications

Co-author of *Farm Work Simplification* (Wiley)

Author of book chapters and Purdue University research bulletins on agricultural economics, farm management, development

Contributor to professional journals

Honors

Sagamore of the Wabash, 2003

Book of Great Teachers, Purdue University, 1999

Nyle C. Brady Award, Consultative Group for International Agricultural Research, Washington, D.C., 1998

Fellow, American Agricultural Economic Association, 1979

Fellow, American Association for the Advancement of Science, 1996 Citation: "For organization and scientific leadership contributing significantly to the creation, management, outreach and impact of the global network of international research centers"

Doctor of Agriculture, *honoris causa*, Purdue University, 1990.

Special assignments

Secretary-Treasurer, 1953–57; Vice President, 1959; President, 1963–64, American Agricultural Economics Association

Faculty member, Stonier Graduate School of Banking, Rutgers University, 1955–65

Consultant, Office State Experiment Station, USDA, Washington, D.C.

Member, Agricultural Board, National Academy of Science, 1966–72

Member, Panel of President's Science Advisory Committee on World Food Supply, Washington D.C., 1966–67

Trustee, Agricultural Development Council (A/D/C), New York, 1962–66; Chairman of the Board, 1982–85

Trustee, International Center for Corn and Wheat Improvement (CIMMYT), Mexico, 1966–72

Trustee, International Agricultural Development Service (IADS), New York, 1968–72

Trustee, International Center for Tropical Agriculture (CIAT), Colombia, 1967–72

Member, Joint Research Committee, Board for International Food and Agricultural Development (BIFAD), Title XII, U.S. Agency for International Development (AID), 1977–79

Vice Chairman, Board of Trustees, International Center for Agricultural Research in the Dry Areas (ICARDA), Beirut, Lebanon, and Aleppo, Syria, 1979–85

Trustee, International Service for National Agricultural Research (ISNAR), The Hague, Netherlands, 1979–84

Trustee, International Food Policy Research Institute (IFPRI), Washington, D.C., 1980–87

Member, Board of Directors, Winrock International Institute for Agricultural Development (WI), Morrilton, Arkansas, and Washington D.C., 1985–93

Chairman, National Research Council Panel for Collaborative Research Support for AID's Sustainable Agriculture and National Resource Management Program, 1990–91

Member, National Research Council Panel on Agricultural Sustainability and the Environment in the Humid Tropics, Washington D.C., 1990–93

International experience

United States delegate to International Conference of Agricultural Economists, England, 1947

Conducted study of market development in Japan, 1960

Technical consultant to Purdue-Brazil Program, 1962

Technical consultant to Ford Foundation and Rockefeller Foundation for agricultural programs in Colombia and Mexico, 1963–65

Approximately one-third time overseas working with agricultural development programs in Latin America, Africa and Asia, 1965–82

Advisory/consulting work including external management reviews of international agricultural centers mentioned above, 1983 and after

Advisory/consulting work including external management reviews of International Livestock Center for Africa (ILCA), Ethiopia, 1986; CIAT, Colombia, 1986; International Rice Research Institute (IRRI), Philippines, 1987; International Laboratory for Research on Animal Diseases (ILRAD), Kenya, 1987; CIMMYT, Mexico, 1987; The International Potato Center (CIP), Peru, 1989; and the Consultative Group for International Agricultural Research (CGIAR), Washington D.C., 1981–2000

About the Editors

Larry L. Murdock, Purdue University distinguished professor emeritus, was born in Linton, Indiana. Mentored and inspired by Lowell Hardin, Murdock's work laid the foundation for the world's first insect-resistant genetically modified seeds and for Bt-cowpea, now in the field in Nigeria. His work also led to the development of the PICS grain storage technology, which is used throughout the world.

Thomas W. Hertel is Distinguished Professor of Agricultural Economics at Purdue University. His research and teaching focuses on international trade, food, and environmental security. He is a 2022 recipient of the Alexander von Humboldt Research Prize, and he serves as the founder and executive director of the Global Trade Analysis Project (GTAP), which now encompasses more than 29,000 researchers in 179 countries.

Gebisa Ejeta is Distinguished Professor of Plant Breeding and Genetics and International Agriculture at Purdue University, and director of the Purdue Center for Global Food Security. He has been highly honored for his significant contributions to science and development. Ejeta was awarded the World Food Prize in 2009, and received the US National Medal of Science, given by President Biden, in 2023.